W9-CFV-509

Jamie + Ina Nason

Presented to

Teyla Trask

From

july 13 2013

Date

God's Wisdom

FOR YOUR

Marriage

by Jack Countryman

A Division of Thomas Nelson Publishers

THOMAS NELSON
Since 1798

NASHVILLE   DALLAS   MEXICO CITY   RIO DE JANEIRO

God's Wisdom for Your Marriage
© 2012 Jack Countryman

All rights reserved. No portion of this book may be reproduced, stored in a retrieval system, or transmitted in any form or by any means—electronic, mechanical, photocopy, recording, scanning, or other—except for brief quotations in critical reviews or articles, without the prior written permission of the publisher.

Published in Nashville, Tennessee, by Thomas Nelson®. Thomas Nelson is a registered trademark of Thomas Nelson, Inc.

Scripture quotations are taken from the NEW KING JAMES VERSION, © 1982 by Thomas Nelson, Inc. Used by permission. All rights reserved.

Thomas Nelson, Inc., titles may be purchased in bulk for educational, business, fund-raising, or sales promotional use. For information, please e-mail SpecialMarkets@ ThomasNelson.com.

ISBN-13: 978-1-4003-2022-6

Printed in China

12 13 14 15 RRD 5 4 3 2 1

www.thomasnelson.com

Contents

GOD'S TRUTH

GOD'S SOLUTIONS

GOD'S DESIRES

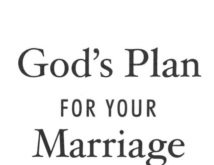

God's Plan

FOR YOUR
Marriage

❧ Pray Together ❧

Most assuredly, I say to you, whatever you ask the Father in My name He will give you. Until now you have asked nothing in My name. Ask, and you will receive, that your joy may be full.

John 16:23–24

Now this is the confidence that we have in Him, that if we ask anything according to His will, He hears us. And if we know that He hears us, whatever we ask, we know that we have the petitions that we have asked of Him.

1 John 5:14–15

Assuredly, I say to you, whatever you bind on earth will be bound in heaven, and whatever you loose on earth will be loosed in heaven. Again I say to you that if two of you agree on earth concerning anything that they ask, it will be done for them by My Father in heaven.

Matthew 18:18–19

If My people who are called by My name will humble themselves, and pray and seek My face, and turn from their wicked ways, then I will hear from heaven, and will forgive their sin and heal their land.

2 Chronicles 7:14

Cast your burden on the LORD,
  And He shall sustain you;
  He shall never permit the righteous to be moved.

Psalm 55:22

I love the LORD, because He has heard
  My voice and my supplications.
Because He has inclined His ear to me,
  Therefore I will call upon Him as long as I live.

Psalm 116:1–2

Rejoice always, pray without ceasing, in everything give thanks; for this is the will of God in Christ Jesus for you.

1 Thessalonians 5:16–18

Humble yourselves under the mighty hand of God, that He may exalt you in due time, casting all your care upon Him, for He cares for you.

1 Peter 5:6–7

Praise God Together

I will sing to the LORD as long as I live;
    I will sing praise to my God while I have my being.
May my meditation be sweet to Him;
    I will be glad in the LORD.

Psalm 104:33–34

You shall fear the LORD your God; you shall serve Him,
and to Him you shall hold fast, and take oaths in His
name. He is your praise, and He is your God, who has
done for you these great and awesome things which your
eyes have seen.

Deuteronomy 10:20–21

Oh, clap your hands, all you peoples!
    Shout to God with the voice of triumph! . . .
Sing praises to God, sing praises!
    Sing praises to our King, sing praises!
For God is the King of all the earth;
    Sing praises with understanding.

Psalm 47:1, 6–7

Let us continually offer the sacrifice of praise to God, that is, the fruit of our lips, giving thanks to His name.

Hebrews 13:15

Because Your lovingkindness is better than life,
My lips shall praise You.
Thus I will bless You while I live;
I will lift up my hands in Your name.
My soul shall be satisfied as with marrow and fatness,
And my mouth shall praise You with joyful lips.

Psalm 63:3–5

Let my mouth be filled with Your praise
And with Your glory all the day....
But I will hope continually,
And will praise You yet more and more.

Psalm 71:8, 14

I will bless the LORD at all times;
His praise shall continually be in my mouth.
My soul shall make its boast in the LORD;
The humble shall hear of it and be glad.
Oh, magnify the LORD with me,
And let us exalt His name together.

Psalm 34:1–3

Make a joyful shout to the LORD, all you lands!
Serve the LORD with gladness;
Come before His presence with singing.
Know that the LORD, He is God;
It is He who has made us, and not we ourselves;
We are His people and the sheep of His pasture.
Enter into His gates with thanksgiving,
And into His courts with praise.
Be thankful to Him, and bless His name.
For the LORD is good;
His mercy is everlasting,
And His truth endures to all generations.

Psalm 100

 Serve God Together

If it seems evil to you to serve the LORD, choose for yourselves this day whom you will serve. . . . But as for me and my house, we will serve the LORD.

Joshua 24:15

What does the LORD your God require of you, but to fear the LORD your God, to walk in all His ways and to love Him, to serve the LORD your God with all your heart and with all your soul?

Deuteronomy 10:12

If you earnestly obey My commandments which I command you today, to love the LORD your God and serve Him with all your heart and with all your soul, then I will give you the rain for your land in its season, the early rain and the latter rain, that you may gather in your grain, your new wine, and your oil. And I will send grass in your fields for your livestock, that you may eat and be filled.

Deuteronomy 11:13–15

Present your bodies a living sacrifice, holy, acceptable to God, which is your reasonable service. And do not be conformed to this world, but be transformed by the renewing of your mind, that you may prove what is that good and acceptable and perfect will of God.

Romans 12:1–2

Take careful heed to do the commandment and the law which Moses the servant of the LORD commanded you, to love the LORD your God, to walk in all His ways, to keep His commandments, to hold fast to Him, and to serve Him with all your heart and with all your soul.

Joshua 22:5

Serve the LORD with gladness;
    Come before His presence with singing.
Know that the LORD, He is God;
    It is He who has made us, and not we ourselves;
    We are His people and the sheep of His pasture.

Psalm 100:2–3

You shall serve the LORD your God, and He will bless your bread and your water.

Exodus 23:25

Be kindly affectionate to one another with brotherly love, in honor giving preference to one another; not lagging in diligence, fervent in spirit, serving the Lord; . . . distributing to the needs of the saints, given to hospitality.

Romans 12:10–11, 13

He has shown you, O man, what is good;
    And what does the LORD require of you
    But to do justly,
    To love mercy,
    And to walk humbly with your God?

Micah 6:8

Draw Closer to God

It is good for me to draw near to God;
   I have put my trust in the Lord God,
   That I may declare all Your works.

Psalm 73:28

The Lord is righteous in all His ways,
   Gracious in all His works.
The Lord is near to all who call upon Him,
   To all who call upon Him in truth.
He will fulfill the desire of those who fear Him;
   He also will hear their cry and save them.

Psalm 145:17–19

As newborn babes, desire the pure milk of the word, that you may grow thereby, if indeed you have tasted that the Lord is gracious.

1 Peter 2:2–3

I bow my knees to the Father of our Lord Jesus Christ, from whom the whole family in heaven and earth is named, that He would grant you, according to the riches of His glory, to be strengthened with might through His Spirit in the inner man, that Christ may dwell in your hearts through faith; that you, being rooted and grounded in love, may be able to comprehend with all the saints what is the width and length and depth and height—to know the love of Christ which passes knowledge; that you may be filled with all the fullness of God.

Ephesians 3:14–19

Meditate on [Jesus' teachings and God's commands]; give yourself entirely to them, that your progress may be evident to all. Take heed to yourself and to the doctrine. Continue in them, for in doing this you will save both yourself and those who hear you.

1 Timothy 4:15–16

Be diligent to present yourself approved to God, a worker who does not need to be ashamed, rightly dividing the word of truth.

2 Timothy 2:15

If anyone cleanses himself from [dishonor], he will be a vessel for honor, sanctified and useful for the Master, prepared for every good work. Flee also youthful lusts; but pursue righteousness, faith, love, peace with those who call on the Lord out of a pure heart.

2 Timothy 2:21–22

Let the wicked forsake his way,
    And the unrighteous man his thoughts;
    Let him return to the LORD,
    And He will have mercy on him;
    And to our God,
    For He will abundantly pardon.

Isaiah 55:7

Because You have been my help,
    Therefore in the shadow of Your wings I will rejoice.
My soul follows close behind You;
    Your right hand upholds me.

Psalm 63:7–8

Stand Strong Together

Two are better than one,
Because they have a good reward for their labor.
For if they fall, one will lift up his companion.
But woe to him who is alone when he falls,
For he has no one to help him up.

Ecclesiastes 4:9–10

A friend loves at all times.

Proverbs 17:17

We do not lose heart. Even though our outward man is perishing, yet the inward man is being renewed day by day. For our light affliction, which is but for a moment, is working for us a far more exceeding and eternal weight of glory, while we do not look at the things which are seen, but at the things which are not seen. For the things which are seen are temporary, but the things which are not seen are eternal.

2 Corinthians 4:16–18

[We] glory in tribulations, knowing that tribulation produces perseverance; and perseverance, character; and character, hope. Now hope does not disappoint, because the love of God has been poured out in our hearts by the Holy Spirit who was given to us.

Romans 5:3–5

If anyone desires to come after Me, let him deny himself, and take up his cross daily, and follow Me. For whoever desires to save his life will lose it, but whoever loses his life for My sake will save it.

Luke 9:23–24

Thanks be to God, who gives us the victory through our Lord Jesus Christ. Therefore, my beloved brethren, be steadfast, immovable, always abounding in the work of the Lord, knowing that your labor is not in vain in the Lord.

1 Corinthians 15:57–58

He who sows to his flesh will of the flesh reap corruption, but he who sows to the Spirit will of the Spirit reap everlasting life. And let us not grow weary while doing good, for in due season we shall reap if we do not lose heart. Therefore, as we have opportunity, let us do good to all, especially to those who are of the household of faith.

Galatians 6:8–10

Do not cast away your confidence, which has great reward. For you have need of endurance, so that after you have done the will of God, you may receive the promise.

Hebrews 10:35–36

I can do all things through Christ who strengthens me.

Philippians 4:13

If we endure,
    We shall also reign with Him.
If we deny Him,
    He also will deny us.
If we are faithless,
    He remains faithful;
He cannot deny Himself.

2 Timothy 2:12–13

God has set the members, each one of them, in the body just as He pleased. And if they were all one member, where would the body be?

But now indeed there are many members, yet one body. And the eye cannot say to the hand, "I have no need of you"; nor again the head to the feet, "I have no need of you." . . . If one member suffers, all the members suffer with it; or if one member is honored, all the members rejoice with it.

1 Corinthians 12:18–21, 26

 Obey God

Behold, I set before you today a blessing and a curse: the blessing, if you obey the commandments of the LORD your God which I command you today; and the curse, if you do not obey the commandments of the LORD your God, but turn aside from the way which I command you today, to go after other gods which you have not known.

Deuteronomy 11:26–28

Oh, that you had heeded My commandments!
Then your peace would have been like a river,
And your righteousness like the waves of the sea.

Isaiah 48:18

Obey My voice, and I will be your God, and you shall be My people. And walk in all the ways that I have commanded you, that it may be well with you.

Jeremiah 7:23

If you love Me, keep My commandments. . . . He who has My commandments and keeps them, it is he who loves Me. And he who loves Me will be loved by My Father, and I will love him and manifest Myself to him.

John 14:15, 21

Teach me to do Your will,
For You are my God;
Your Spirit is good.
Lead me in the land of uprightness.

Psalm 143:10

Moses called all Israel, and said to them: "Hear, O Israel, the statutes and judgments which I speak in your hearing today, that you may learn them and be careful to observe them. . . . You shall be careful to do as the LORD your God has commanded you; you shall not turn aside to the right hand or to the left. You shall walk in all the ways which the LORD your God has commanded you, that you may live and that it may be well with you, and that you may prolong your days in the land which you shall possess."

Deuteronomy 5:1, 32–33

Now by this we know that we know Him, if we keep His commandments. He who says, "I know Him," and does not keep His commandments, is a liar, and the truth is not in him. But whoever keeps His word, truly the love of God is perfected in him. By this we know that we are in Him. He who says he abides in Him ought himself also to walk just as He walked.

1 John 2:3–6

So if you walk in My ways, to keep My statutes and My commandments, as your father David walked, then I will lengthen your days.

1 Kings 3:14

Follow God Together

Trust in the LORD with all your heart,
And lean not on your own understanding;
In all your ways acknowledge Him,
And He shall direct your paths.

Proverbs 3:5–6

Let the word of Christ dwell in you richly in all wisdom, teaching and admonishing one another in psalms and hymns and spiritual songs, singing with grace in your hearts to the Lord.

Colossians 3:16

Let Your hand become my help,
For I have chosen Your precepts.
I long for Your salvation, O LORD,
And Your law is my delight.
Let my soul live, and it shall praise You;
And let Your judgments help me.

Psalm 119:173–175

But He who looks into the perfect law of liberty and continues in it, and is not a forgetful hearer but a doer of the work, this one will be blessed in what he does.

James 1:25

Through Your precepts I get understanding;
    Therefore I hate every false way.
Your word is a lamp to my feet
    And a light to my path.
I have sworn and confirmed
    That I will keep Your righteous judgments.

Psalm 119:104–106

Do not forget my law,
    But let your heart keep my commands;
For length of days and long life
    And peace they will add to you.

Proverbs 3:1–2

Trust in the LORD, and do good;
    Dwell in the land, and feed on His faithfulness.
Delight yourself also in the Lord,
    And He shall give you the desires of your heart.
Commit your way to the LORD,
    Trust also in Him,
    And He shall bring it to pass.

Psalm 37:3–5

God's
Guidance

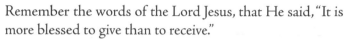 For Your Finances

Remember the words of the Lord Jesus, that He said, "It is more blessed to give than to receive."

Acts 20:35

Command those who are rich in this present age not to be haughty, nor to trust in uncertain riches but in the living God, who gives us richly all things to enjoy. Let them do good, that they be rich in good works, ready to give, willing to share, storing up for themselves a good foundation for the time to come, that they may lay hold on eternal life.

1 Timothy 6:17–19

You will prosper, if you take care to fulfill the statutes and judgments with which the Lord charged Moses concerning Israel. Be strong and of good courage; do not fear nor be dismayed. Indeed I have taken much trouble to prepare for the house of the Lord one hundred thousand talents of gold and one million talents of silver, and bronze and iron beyond measure, for it is so abundant. I have prepared timber and stone also, and you may add to them.

1 Chronicles 22:13–14

Trust in the LORD with all your heart,
   And lean not on your own understanding;
In all your ways acknowledge Him,
   And He shall direct your paths.

Do not be wise in your own eyes;
   Fear the LORD and depart from evil.
It will be health to your flesh,
   And strength to your bones.

Honor the LORD with your possessions,
   And with the firstfruits of all your increase;
So your barns will be filled with plenty,
   And your vats will overflow with new wine.

Proverbs 3:5–10

He who sows sparingly will also reap sparingly, and he who sows bountifully will also reap bountifully. So let each one give as he purposes in his heart, not grudgingly or of necessity; for God loves a cheerful giver.

2 Corinthians 9:6–7

Give, and it will be given to you: good measure, pressed down, shaken together, and running over will be put into your bosom. For with the same measure that you use, it will be measured back to you.

Luke 6:38

You shall remember the Lord your God, for it is He who gives you power to get wealth, that He may establish His covenant which He swore to your fathers, as it is this day.

Deuteronomy 8:18

Blessed is the man who fears the Lord,
Who delights greatly in His commandments.
His descendants will be mighty on earth;
The generation of the upright will be blessed.
Wealth and riches will be in his house,
And his righteousness endures forever.

Psalm 112:1–3

"Bring all the tithes into the storehouse,
That there may be food in My house,
And try Me now in this,"
Says the Lord of hosts,
"If I will not open for you the windows of heaven
And pour out for you such blessing
That there will not be room enough to receive it."

Malachi 3:10

To Know His Will

If you extend your soul to the hungry
    And satisfy the afflicted soul,
    Then your light shall dawn in the darkness,
    And your darkness shall be as the noonday.
The Lord will guide you continually,
    And satisfy your soul in drought,
    And strengthen your bones;
    You shall be like a watered garden,
    And like a spring of water, whose waters do not fail.

Isaiah 58:10–11

When He, the Spirit of truth, has come, He will guide you into all truth; for He will not speak on His own authority, but whatever He hears He will speak; and He will tell you things to come. He will glorify Me, for He will take of what is Mine and declare it to you. All things that the Father has are Mine. Therefore I said that He will take of Mine and declare it to you.

John 16:13–15

He found him in a desert land
    And in the wasteland, a howling wilderness;
    He encircled him, He instructed him,
    He kept him as the apple of His eye.
As an eagle stirs up its nest,
    Hovers over its young,
    Spreading out its wings, taking them up,
    Carrying them on its wings,
So the Lord alone led him,
    And there was no foreign god with him.

Deuteronomy 32:10–12

A man's heart plans his way,
    But the Lord directs his steps. . . .
How much better to get wisdom than gold!
    And to get understanding is to be chosen rather
            than silver. . . .
He who heeds the word wisely will find good,
    And whoever trusts in the Lord, happy is he.
The wise in heart will be called prudent,
    And sweetness of the lips increases learning. . . .
The heart of the wise teaches his mouth,
    And adds learning to his lips. . . .
The lot is cast into the lap,
    But its every decision is from the Lord.

Proverbs 16:9, 16, 20–21, 23, 33

For this is God,
    Our God forever and ever;
    He will be our guide
    Even to death.

Psalm 48:14

This is the will of God, your sanctification: that you should abstain from sexual immorality; that each of you should know how to possess his own vessel in sanctification and honor, not in passion of lust, like the Gentiles who do not know God; that no one should take advantage of and defraud his brother in this matter, because the Lord is the avenger of all such, as we also forewarned you and testified. For God did not call us to uncleanness, but in holiness. Therefore he who rejects this does not reject man, but God, who has also given us His Holy Spirit.

1 Thessalonians 4:3–8

Bondservants, be obedient to those who are your masters according to the flesh, with fear and trembling, in sincerity of heart, as to Christ; not with eyeservice, as men-pleasers, but as bondservants of Christ, doing the will of God from the heart, with goodwill doing service, as to the Lord, and not to men, knowing that whatever good anyone does, he will receive the same from the Lord.

Ephesians 6:5–8

I beseech you therefore, brethren, by the mercies of God, that you present your bodies a living sacrifice, holy, acceptable to God, which is your reasonable service. And do not be conformed to this world, but be transformed by the renewing of your mind, that you may prove what is that good and acceptable and perfect will of God.

Romans 12:1–2

For Your Marriage

The Lord God said, "It is not good that man should be alone; I will make him a helper comparable to him." . . . Therefore a man shall leave his father and mother and be joined to his wife, and they shall become one flesh.

Genesis 2:18, 24

He who finds a wife finds a good thing,
And obtains favor from the Lord.

Proverbs 18:22

Because of sexual immorality, let each man have his own wife, and let each woman have her own husband. Let the husband render to his wife the affection due her, and likewise also the wife to her husband. The wife does not have authority over her own body, but the husband does. And likewise the husband does not have authority over his own body, but the wife does.

1 Corinthians 7:2–4

Wives, submit to your own husbands, as to the Lord. For the husband is head of the wife, as also Christ is head of the church; and He is the Savior of the body. Therefore, just as the church is subject to Christ, so let the wives be to their own husbands in everything.

Husbands, love your wives, just as Christ also loved the church and gave Himself for her, that He might sanctify and cleanse her with the washing of water by the word, that He might present her to Himself a glorious church, not having spot or wrinkle or any such thing, but that she should be holy and without blemish. So husbands ought to love their own wives as their own bodies; he who loves his wife loves himself. For no one ever hated his own flesh, but nourishes and cherishes it, just as the Lord does the church. For we are members of His body, of His flesh and of His bones. "For this reason a man shall leave his father and mother and be joined to his wife, and the two shall become one flesh."

Ephesians 5:22–31

Marriage is honorable among all, and the bed undefiled; but fornicators and adulterers God will judge. Let your conduct be without covetousness; be content with such things as you have. For He Himself has said, "I will never leave you nor forsake you."

Hebrews 13:4–5

He who is married cares about the things of the world—how he may please his wife. . . . The unmarried woman cares about the things of the Lord, that she may be holy both in body and in spirit. But she who is married cares about the things of the world—how she may please her husband.

1 Corinthians 7:33–34

Neither is man independent of woman, nor woman independent of man, in the Lord. For as woman came from man, even so man also comes through woman; but all things are from God.

1 Corinthians 11:11–12

For Your Family

These words which I command you today shall be in your heart. You shall teach them diligently to your children, and shall talk of them when you sit in your house, when you walk by the way, when you lie down, and when you rise up.

Deuteronomy 6:6–7

The father of the righteous will greatly rejoice,
And he who begets a wise child will delight in him.

Proverbs 23:24

Fathers, do not provoke your children to wrath, but bring them up in the training and admonition of the Lord.

Ephesians 6:4

Let all bitterness, wrath, anger, clamor, and evil speaking be put away from you, with all malice. And be kind to one another, tenderhearted, forgiving one another, even as God in Christ forgave you.

Ephesians 4:31–32

Fear the Lord, serve Him in sincerity and in truth, and put away the gods which your fathers served on the other side of the River and in Egypt. Serve the Lord! . . . Choose for yourselves this day whom you will serve. . . . But as for me and my house, we will serve the Lord.

Joshua 24:14–15

Train up a child in the way he should go,
    And when he is old he will not depart from it.

Proverbs 22:6

Correct your son, and he will give you rest;
    Yes, he will give delight to your soul.

Proverbs 29:17

The mercy of the Lord is from everlasting to everlasting
    On those who fear Him,
    And His righteousness to children's children,
To such as keep His covenant,
    And to those who remember His commandments to
          do them.

Psalm 103:17–18

Fathers, do not provoke your children, lest they become discouraged.

Colossians 3:21

🌿 For Being a Husband 🌿

He who finds a wife finds a good thing,
  And obtains favor from the LORD.

Proverbs 18:22

Live joyfully with the wife whom you love all the days of your vain life which He has given you under the sun.

Ecclesiastes 9:9

Husbands, likewise, dwell with [your wife] with understanding, giving honor to the wife, as to the weaker vessel, and as being heirs together of the grace of life, that your prayers may not be hindered.

1 Peter 3:7

Let your fountain be blessed,
  And rejoice with the wife of your youth.
As a loving deer and a graceful doe,
  Let her breasts satisfy you at all times;
  And always be enraptured with her love.

Proverbs 5:18–19

Husbands, love your wives, just as Christ also loved the church and gave Himself for her, that He might sanctify and cleanse her with the washing of water by the word, that He might present her to Himself a glorious church, not having spot or wrinkle or any such thing, but that she should be holy and without blemish. So husbands ought to love their own wives as their own bodies; he who loves his wife loves himself. For no one ever hated his own flesh, but nourishes and cherishes it, just as the Lord does the church. For we are members of His body, of His flesh and of His bones. "For this reason a man shall leave his father and mother and be joined to his wife, and the two shall become one flesh." . . . Nevertheless let each one of you in particular so love his own wife as himself, and let the wife see that she respects her husband.

Ephesians 5:25–31, 33

Because of sexual immorality, let each man have his own wife, and let each woman have her own husband. Let the husband render to his wife the affection due her, and likewise also the wife to her husband. The wife does not have authority over her own body, but the husband does. And likewise the husband does not have authority over his own body, but the wife does.

1 Corinthians 7:2–4

Happy is the man who finds wisdom,
    And the man who gains understanding;
For her proceeds are better than the profits of silver,
    And her gain than fine gold.
She is more precious than rubies,
    And all the things you may desire cannot compare
            with her.
Length of days is in her right hand,
    In her left hand riches and honor.
Her ways are ways of pleasantness,
    And all her paths are peace.
She is a tree of life to those who take hold of her,
    And happy are all who retain her.

Proverbs 3:13–18

Husbands, love your wives and do not be bitter toward them.

Colossians 3:19

Houses and riches are an inheritance from fathers,
    But a prudent wife is from the LORD.

Proverbs 19:14

For Being a Wife

Wives, submit to your own husbands, as is fitting in the Lord.

Colossians 3:18

Because of sexual immorality, let each man have his own wife, and let each woman have her own husband. Let the husband render to his wife the affection due her, and likewise also the wife to her husband. The wife does not have authority over her own body, but the husband does. And likewise the husband does not have authority over his own body, but the wife does.

1 Corinthians 7:2–4

A wife is not to depart from her husband.

1 Corinthians 7:10

Houses and riches are an inheritance from fathers,
But a prudent wife is from the LORD.

Proverbs 19:14

Wives, likewise, be submissive to your own husbands, that even if some do not obey the word, they, without a word, may be won by the conduct of their wives, when they observe your chaste conduct accompanied by fear. Do not let your adornment be merely outward—arranging the hair, wearing gold, or putting on fine apparel—rather let it be the hidden person of the heart, with the incorruptible beauty of a gentle and quiet spirit, which is very precious in the sight of God. For in this manner, in former times, the holy women who trusted in God also adorned themselves, being submissive to their own husbands, as Sarah obeyed Abraham, calling him lord, whose daughters you are if you do good and are not afraid with any terror.

1 Peter 3:1–6

The wicked flee when no one pursues,
But the righteous are bold as a lion.
Because of the transgression of a land, many are its princes;
But by a man of understanding and knowledge
Right will be prolonged.
A poor man who oppresses the poor
Is like a driving rain which leaves no food.
Those who forsake the law praise the wicked,
But such as keep the law contend with them.

Proverbs 28:1–4

Who can find a virtuous wife?
　　For her worth is far above rubies.
The heart of her husband safely trusts her;
　　So he will have no lack of gain.
She does him good and not evil
　　All the days of her life. . . .

Her children rise up and call her blessed;
　　Her husband also, and he praises her:
"Many daughters have done well,
　　But you excel them all."
Charm is deceitful and beauty is passing,
　　But a woman who fears the Lord, she shall be praised.
Give her of the fruit of her hands,
　　And let her own works praise her in the gates.
Proverbs 31:10–12, 28–31

An excellent wife is the crown of her husband,
　　But she who causes shame is like rottenness in his bones.
Proverbs 12:4

God's
Provision

For Your Needs

My God shall supply all your need according to His riches in glory by Christ Jesus.

Philippians 4:19

Do not worry, saying, "What shall we eat?" or "What shall we drink?" or "What shall we wear?" For after all these things the Gentiles seek. For your heavenly Father knows that you need all these things. But seek first the kingdom of God and His righteousness, and all these things shall be added to you.

Matthew 6:31–33

I have been young, and now am old;
    Yet I have not seen the righteous forsaken,
    Nor his descendants begging bread.
He is ever merciful, and lends;
    And his descendants are blessed.

Psalm 37:25–26

I will bless the LORD at all times;
   His praise shall continually be in my mouth.
My soul shall make its boast in the LORD;
   The humble shall hear of it and be glad.
Oh, magnify the LORD with me,
   And let us exalt His name together. . . .

The young lions lack and suffer hunger;
   But those who seek the LORD shall not lack any
         good thing.

Psalm 34:1–3, 10

Let each one give as he purposes in his heart, not grudgingly or of necessity; for God loves a cheerful giver. And God is able to make all grace abound toward you, that you, always having all sufficiency in all things, may have an abundance for every good work.

2 Corinthians 9:7–8

Give, and it will be given to you: good measure, pressed down, shaken together, and running over will be put into your bosom. For with the same measure that you use, it will be measured back to you.

Luke 6:38

The LORD will grant you plenty of goods, in the fruit of your body, in the increase of your livestock, and in the produce of your ground, in the land of which the LORD swore to your fathers to give you. The LORD will open to you His good treasure, the heavens, to give the rain to your land in its season, and to bless all the work of your hand. You shall lend to many nations, but you shall not borrow.

Deuteronomy 28:11–12

Of Health

If you extend your soul to the hungry
    And satisfy the afflicted soul,
    Then your light shall dawn in the darkness,
    And your darkness shall be as the noonday.
The Lord will guide you continually,
    And satisfy your soul in drought,
    And strengthen your bones;
    You shall be like a watered garden,
    And like a spring of water, whose waters do not fail.

Isaiah 58:10–11

Is anyone among you sick? Let him call for the elders of the church, and let them pray over him, anointing him with oil in the name of the Lord. And the prayer of faith will save the sick, and the Lord will raise him up.

James 5:14–15

Heal me, O Lord, and I shall be healed;
    Save me, and I shall be saved,
    For You are my praise.

Jeremiah 17:14

Blessed is the man to whom the LORD does not
impute iniquity,
And in whose spirit there is no deceit.
When I kept silent, my bones grew old
Through my groaning all the day long.
For day and night Your hand was heavy upon me;
My vitality was turned into the drought of summer.
I acknowledged my sin to You,
And my iniquity I have not hidden.
I said, "I will confess my transgressions to the LORD,"
And You forgave the iniquity of my sin.

Psalm 32:2–5

Do not be wise in your own eyes;
Fear the LORD and depart from evil.
It will be health to your flesh,
And strength to your bones.

Proverbs 3:7–8

You will keep him in perfect peace,
Whose mind is stayed on You,
Because he trusts in You.
Trust in the LORD forever,
For in YAH, the LORD, is everlasting strength.

Isaiah 26:3–4

We know that if our earthly house, this tent, is destroyed, we have a building from God, a house not made with hands, eternal in the heavens. For in this we groan, earnestly desiring to be clothed with our habitation which is from heaven, if indeed, having been clothed, we shall not be found naked. For we who are in this tent groan, being burdened, not because we want to be unclothed, but further clothed, that mortality may be swallowed up by life.

2 Corinthians 5:1–4

The heart of the wise teaches his mouth,
    And adds learning to his lips.
Pleasant words are like a honeycomb,
    Sweetness to the soul and health to the bones.

Proverbs 16:23–24

My son, give attention to my words;
    Incline your ear to my sayings.
Do not let them depart from your eyes;
    Keep them in the midst of your heart;
For they are life to those who find them,
    And health to all their flesh.
Keep your heart with all diligence,
    For out of it spring the issues of life.

Proverbs 4:20–23

Have mercy on me, O Lord, for I am in trouble;
　My eye wastes away with grief,
　Yes, my soul and my body!
For my life is spent with grief,
　And my years with sighing;
　My strength fails because of my iniquity,
　And my bones waste away.

Psalm 31:9–10

 Of Protection

Do not be afraid of sudden terror,
Nor of trouble from the wicked when it comes;
For the LORD will be your confidence,
And will keep your foot from being caught.

Proverbs 3:25–26

No evil shall befall you,
Nor shall any plague come near your dwelling;
For He shall give His angels charge over you,
To keep you in all your ways.

Psalm 91:10–11

Whenever I am afraid,
I will trust in You.
In God (I will praise His word),
In God I have put my trust;
I will not fear.
What can flesh do to me?

Psalm 56:3–4

He who dwells in the secret place of the Most High
    Shall abide under the shadow of the Almighty.
I will say of the LORD, "He is my refuge and my fortress;
    My God, in Him I will trust."
Surely He shall deliver you from the snare of the fowler
    And from the perilous pestilence.
He shall cover you with His feathers,
    And under His wings you shall take refuge;
    His truth shall be your shield and buckler.
You shall not be afraid of the terror by night,
    Nor of the arrow that flies by day,
Nor of the pestilence that walks in darkness,
    Nor of the destruction that lays waste at noonday.
A thousand may fall at your side,
    And ten thousand at your right hand;
    But it shall not come near you.

Psalm 91:1–7

Oh, love the LORD, all you His saints!
    For the LORD preserves the faithful,
    And fully repays the proud person.
Be of good courage,
    And He shall strengthen your heart,
    All you who hope in the LORD.

Psalm 31:23–24

Thus says the LORD, who created you, O Jacob,
    And He who formed you, O Israel:
    "Fear not, for I have redeemed you;
    I have called you by your name;
    You are Mine.
When you pass through the waters, I will be with you;
    And through the rivers, they shall not overflow you.
    When you walk through the fire, you shall not be burned,
    Nor shall the flame scorch you.
For I am the LORD your God,
    The Holy One of Israel, your Savior.

Isaiah 43:1–3

The LORD is my light and my salvation;
    Whom shall I fear?
    The LORD is the strength of my life;
    Of whom shall I be afraid?
When the wicked came against me
    To eat up my flesh,
    My enemies and foes,
    They stumbled and fell.
Though an army may encamp against me,
    My heart shall not fear;
    Though war may rise against me,
    In this I will be confident.

Psalm 27:1–3

"In righteousness you shall be established;
    You shall be far from oppression, for you shall not fear;
    And from terror, for it shall not come near you.
    Indeed they shall surely assemble, but not because
                of Me.
    Whoever assembles against you shall fall for your sake. . . .
No weapon formed against you shall prosper,
    And every tongue which rises against you in judgment
    You shall condemn.
    This is the heritage of the servants of the LORD,
    And their righteousness is from Me,"
    Says the LORD.

Isaiah 54:14–15, 17

I am with you always, even to the end of the age.

Matthew 28:20

 Of Strength

He gives power to the weak,
    And to those who have no might He increases strength.
Even the youths shall faint and be weary,
    And the young men shall utterly fall,
But those who wait on the LORD
    Shall renew their strength;
    They shall mount up with wings like eagles,
    They shall run and not be weary,
    They shall walk and not faint.

Isaiah 40:29–31

[We] do not cease to pray for you, and to ask that you may be filled with the knowledge of His will in all wisdom and spiritual understanding; that you may walk worthy of the Lord, fully pleasing Him, being fruitful in every good work and increasing in the knowledge of God; strengthened with all might, according to His glorious power, for all patience and longsuffering with joy; giving thanks to the Father who has qualified us to be partakers of the inheritance of the saints in the light.

Colossians 1:9–12

I will love You, O Lord, my strength.
The Lord is my rock and my fortress and my deliverer;
My God, my strength, in whom I will trust;
My shield and the horn of my salvation, my stronghold.
I will call upon the Lord, who is worthy to be praised;
So shall I be saved from my enemies.

Psalm 18:1–3

Fear not, for I am with you;
Be not dismayed, for I am your God.
I will strengthen you,
Yes, I will help you,
I will uphold you with My righteous right hand.

Isaiah 41:10

Be strong in the Lord and in the power of His might.
Put on the whole armor of God, that you may be able to
stand against the wiles of the devil. For we do not wrestle
against flesh and blood, but against principalities, against
powers, against the rulers of the darkness of this age,
against spiritual hosts of wickedness in the heavenly places.
Therefore take up the whole armor of God, that you may
be able to withstand in the evil day, and having done all, to
stand.

Ephesians 6:10–13

Wisdom is with aged men,
  And with length of days, understanding.
With [God] are wisdom and strength,
  He has counsel and understanding.
If He breaks a thing down, it cannot be rebuilt;
  If He imprisons a man, there can be no release.
If He withholds the waters, they dry up;
  If He sends them out, they overwhelm the earth.
With Him are strength and prudence.
  The deceived and the deceiver are His.

Job 12:12–16

The LORD sat enthroned at the Flood,
  And the LORD sits as King forever.
The LORD will give strength to His people;
  The LORD will bless His people with peace.

Psalm 29:10–11

Of Wisdom

Happy is the man who finds wisdom,
    And the man who gains understanding;
For her proceeds are better than the profits of silver,
    And her gain than fine gold.
She is more precious than rubies,
    And all the things you may desire cannot compare
        with her.
Length of days is in her right hand,
    In her left hand riches and honor.
Her ways are ways of pleasantness,
    And all her paths are peace.
She is a tree of life to those who take hold of her,
    And happy are all who retain her.

Proverbs 3:13–18

Let the word of Christ dwell in you richly in all wisdom,
teaching and admonishing one another in psalms and
hymns and spiritual songs, singing with grace in your hearts
to the Lord.

Colossians 3:16

My son, if you receive my words,
    And treasure my commands within you,
So that you incline your ear to wisdom,
    And apply your heart to understanding;
Yes, if you cry out for discernment,
    And lift up your voice for understanding,
If you seek her as silver,
    And search for her as for hidden treasures;
Then you will understand the fear of the LORD,
    And find the knowledge of God.
For the LORD gives wisdom;
    From His mouth come knowledge and understanding;
He stores up sound wisdom for the upright;
    He is a shield to those who walk uprightly.

Proverbs 2:1–7

I have taught you in the way of wisdom;
    I have led you in right paths.
When you walk, your steps will not be hindered,
    And when you run, you will not stumble.
Take firm hold of instruction, do not let go;
    Keep her, for she is your life.

Proverbs 4:11–13

If any of you lacks wisdom, let him ask of God, who gives to all liberally and without reproach, and it will be given to him.

James 1:5

Trust in the LORD with all your heart,
    And lean not on your own understanding;
In all your ways acknowledge Him,
    And He shall direct your paths.

Proverbs 3:5–6

[Enemies of the gospel] will lay their hands on you and persecute you, delivering you up to the synagogues and prisons. You will be brought before kings and rulers for My name's sake. But it will turn out for you as an occasion for testimony. Therefore settle it in your hearts not to meditate beforehand on what you will answer; for I will give you a mouth and wisdom which all your adversaries will not be able to contradict or resist.

Luke 21:12–15

Of Patience

Be patient, brethren, until the coming of the Lord. See how the farmer waits for the precious fruit of the earth, waiting patiently for it until it receives the early and latter rain. You also be patient. Establish your hearts, for the coming of the Lord is at hand.

James 5:7–8

Whatever things were written before were written for our learning, that we through the patience and comfort of the Scriptures might have hope. Now may the God of patience and comfort grant you to be like-minded toward one another, according to Christ Jesus, that you may with one mind and one mouth glorify the God and Father of our Lord Jesus Christ.

Romans 15:4–6

My brethren, count it all joy when you fall into various trials, knowing that the testing of your faith produces patience. But let patience have its perfect work, that you may be perfect and complete, lacking nothing.

James 1:2–4

God is not unjust to forget your work and labor of love which you have shown toward His name, in that you have ministered to the saints, and do minister. And we desire that each one of you show the same diligence to the full assurance of hope until the end, that you do not become sluggish, but imitate those who through faith and patience inherit the promises.

Hebrews 6:10–12

The ones that fell on the good ground are those who, having heard the word with a noble and good heart, keep it and bear fruit with patience.

Luke 8:15

Be kindly affectionate to one another with brotherly love, in honor giving preference to one another; not lagging in diligence, fervent in spirit, serving the Lord; rejoicing in hope, patient in tribulation, continuing steadfastly in prayer.

Romans 12:10–12

Now we exhort you, brethren, warn those who are unruly, comfort the fainthearted, uphold the weak, be patient with all. See that no one renders evil for evil to anyone, but always pursue what is good both for yourselves and for all.

1 Thessalonians 5:14–15

O man of God . . . pursue righteousness, godliness, faith, love, patience, gentleness. Fight the good fight of faith, lay hold on eternal life, to which you were also called and have confessed the good confession in the presence of many witnesses.

1 Timothy 6:11–12

The fruit of the Spirit is love, joy, peace, longsuffering, kindness, goodness, faithfulness, gentleness, self-control.

Galatians 5:22–23

Of Courage

Be strong and of good courage; do not be afraid, nor be dismayed, for the Lord your God is with you wherever you go.

Joshua 1:9

Wait on the Lord;
  Be of good courage,
  And He shall strengthen your heart;
  Wait, I say, on the Lord!

Psalm 27:14

Be strong and of good courage, do not fear nor be afraid . . . for the Lord your God, He is the One who goes with you. He will not leave you nor forsake you.

Deuteronomy 31:6

I am with you always, even to the end of the age.

Matthew 28:20

The name of the Lord is a strong tower;
  The righteous run to it and are safe.

Proverbs 18:10

Let not your heart be troubled; you believe in God, believe also in Me.

John 14:1

God is our refuge and strength,
   A very present help in trouble.
Therefore we will not fear,
   Even though the earth be removed,
      And though the mountains be carried into the midst of
      the sea;
Though its waters roar and be troubled,
   Though the mountains shake with its swelling. Selah

There is a river whose streams shall make glad the city
                     of God,
   The holy place of the tabernacle of the Most High.
God is in the midst of her, she shall not be moved;
   God shall help her, just at the break of dawn.

Psalm 46:1–5

Be strong and courageous; do not be afraid nor dismayed before the king of Assyria, nor before all the multitude that is with him; for there are more with us than with him. With him is an arm of flesh; but with us is the LORD our God, to help us and to fight our battles.

2 Chronicles 32:7–8

🌿 Of Joy 🌿

Let all those rejoice who put their trust in You;
    Let them ever shout for joy, because You defend them;
    Let those also who love Your name
    Be joyful in You.
For You, O Lord, will bless the righteous;
    With favor You will surround him as with a shield.

Psalm 5:11–12

Sing praise to the Lord, you saints of His,
    And give thanks at the remembrance of His holy name.
For His anger is but for a moment,
    His favor is for life;
    Weeping may endure for a night,
    But joy comes in the morning.

Psalm 30:4–5

Restore to me the joy of Your salvation,
    And uphold me by Your generous Spirit.
Then I will teach transgressors Your ways,
    And sinners shall be converted to You.

Psalm 51:12–13

The fruit of the Spirit is love, joy, peace, longsuffering, kindness, goodness, faithfulness, gentleness, self-control.

Galatians 5:22–23

So the ransomed of the LORD shall return,
 And come to Zion with singing,
 With everlasting joy on their heads.
 They shall obtain joy and gladness,
Sorrow and sighing shall flee away.

Isaiah 51:11

If you keep My commandments, you will abide in My love, just as I have kept My Father's commandments and abide in His love. These things I have spoken to you, that My joy may remain in you, and that your joy may be full.

John 15:10–11

Since we are surrounded by so great a cloud of witnesses, let us lay aside every weight, and the sin which so easily ensnares us, and let us run with endurance the race that is set before us, looking unto Jesus, the author and finisher of our faith, who for the joy that was set before Him endured the cross, despising the shame, and has sat down at the right hand of the throne of God.

Hebrews 12:1–2

In this you greatly rejoice, though now for a little while, if need be, you have been grieved by various trials, that the genuineness of your faith, being much more precious than gold that perishes, though it is tested by fire, may be found to praise, honor, and glory at the revelation of Jesus Christ, whom having not seen you love. Though now you do not see Him, yet believing, you rejoice with joy inexpressible and full of glory, receiving the end of your faith—the salvation of your souls.

1 Peter 1:6–9

 Of Comfort

Blessed be the God and Father of our Lord Jesus Christ, the Father of mercies and God of all comfort, who comforts us in all our tribulation, that we may be able to comfort those who are in any trouble, with the comfort with which we ourselves are comforted by God.

2 Corinthians 1:3–4

You, who have shown me great and severe troubles,
    Shall revive me again,
    And bring me up again from the depths of the earth.
You shall increase my greatness,
    And comfort me on every side.

Also with the lute I will praise You—
    And Your faithfulness, O my God!
    To You I will sing with the harp,
    O Holy One of Israel.
My lips shall greatly rejoice when I sing to You,
    And my soul, which You have redeemed.

Psalm 71:20–23

I know, O LORD, that Your judgments are right,
    And that in faithfulness You have afflicted me.
Let, I pray, Your merciful kindness be for my comfort,
    According to Your word to Your servant.

Psalm 119:75–76

When you pass through the waters, I will be with you;
    And through the rivers, they shall not overflow you.
    When you walk through the fire, you shall not be burned,
    Nor shall the flame scorch you.
    For I am the LORD your God,
    The Holy One of Israel, your Savior.

Isaiah 43:2–3

For the LORD will comfort Zion,
    He will comfort all her waste places;
    He will make her wilderness like Eden,
    And her desert like the garden of the Lord;
    Joy and gladness will be found in it,
    Thanksgiving and the voice of melody.

Isaiah 51:3

Whatever things were written before were written for our learning, that we through the patience and comfort of the Scriptures might have hope.

Romans 15:4

For thus says the LORD:
    "Behold, I will extend peace to her like a river,
    And the glory of the Gentiles like a flowing stream.
    Then you shall feed;
    On her sides shall you be carried,
    And be dandled on her knees.
    As one whom his mother comforts,
    So I will comfort you;
    And you shall be comforted in Jerusalem."

Isaiah 66:12–13

If there is any consolation in Christ, if any comfort of love, if any fellowship of the Spirit, if any affection and mercy, fulfill my joy by being like-minded, having the same love, being of one accord, of one mind. Let nothing be done through selfish ambition or conceit, but in lowliness of mind let each esteem others better than himself.

Philippians 2:1–3

 Of Peace

Peace I leave with you, My peace I give to you; not as the world gives do I give to you. Let not your heart be troubled, neither let it be afraid.

John 14:27

For you shall go out with joy,
    And be led out with peace;
    The mountains and the hills
    Shall break forth into singing before you,
    And all the trees of the field shall clap their hands.

Isaiah 55:12

Walk worthy of the calling with which you were called . . . endeavoring to keep the unity of the Spirit in the bond of peace. There is one body and one Spirit, just as you were called in one hope of your calling; one Lord, one faith, one baptism; one God and Father of all, who is above all, and through all, and in you all.

Ephesians 4:1, 3–6

You will keep him in perfect peace,
    Whose mind is stayed on You,
    Because he trusts in You.
    Trust in the Lord forever,
    For in Yah, the Lord, is everlasting strength.

Isaiah 26:3–4

Put on love, which is the bond of perfection. And let the peace of God rule in your hearts, to which also you were called in one body; and be thankful.

Colossians 3:14–15

Those who live according to the flesh set their minds on the things of the flesh, but those who live according to the Spirit, the things of the Spirit. For to be carnally minded is death, but to be spiritually minded is life and peace.

Romans 8:5–6

[Christ Jesus] Himself is our peace, who has made both [Gentiles and Israel] one, and has broken down the middle wall of separation, having abolished in His flesh the enmity, that is, the law of commandments contained in ordinances, so as to create in Himself one new man from the two, thus making peace.

Ephesians 2:14–15

Be anxious for nothing, but in everything by prayer and supplication, with thanksgiving, let your requests be made known to God; and the peace of God, which surpasses all understanding, will guard your hearts and minds through Christ Jesus.

Philippians 4:6–7

God's
Blessings

His Love

When we were still without strength, in due time Christ died for the ungodly. For scarcely for a righteous man will one die; yet perhaps for a good man someone would even dare to die. But God demonstrates His own love toward us, in that while we were still sinners, Christ died for us.

Romans 5:6–8

There is no fear in love; but perfect love casts out fear, because fear involves torment. But he who fears has not been made perfect in love. We love Him because He first loved us.

1 John 4:18–19

Jesus answered and said to [Judas], "If anyone loves Me, he will keep My word; and My Father will love him, and We will come to him and make Our home with him."

John 14:23

The fruit of the Spirit is love.

Galatians 5:22–23

By this we know love, because He laid down His life for us. And we also ought to lay down our lives for the brethren.

1 John 3:16

God so loved the world that He gave His only begotten Son, that whoever believes in Him should not perish but have everlasting life. For God did not send His Son into the world to condemn the world, but that the world through Him might be saved.

John 3:16–17

This is the love of God, that we keep His commandments. And His commandments are not burdensome. For whatever is born of God overcomes the world. And this is the victory that has overcome the world—our faith. Who is he who overcomes the world, but he who believes that Jesus is the Son of God?

1 John 5:3–5

The love of Christ compels us, because we judge thus: that if One died for all, then all died; and He died for all, that those who live should live no longer for themselves, but for Him who died for them and rose again.

2 Corinthians 5:14–15

I bow my knees to the Father of our Lord Jesus Christ . . . that Christ may dwell in your hearts through faith; that you, being rooted and grounded in love, may be able to comprehend with all the saints what is the width and length and depth and height—to know the love of Christ which passes knowledge; that you may be filled with all the fullness of God.

Ephesians 3:14, 17–19

If God is for us, who can be against us? . . . I am persuaded that neither death nor life, nor angels nor principalities nor powers, nor things present nor things to come, nor height nor depth, nor any other created thing, shall be able to separate us from the love of God which is in Christ Jesus our Lord.

Romans 8:31, 38–39

His Mercy

We do not have a High Priest who cannot sympathize with our weaknesses, but was in all points tempted as we are, yet without sin. Let us therefore come boldly to the throne of grace, that we may obtain mercy and find grace to help in time of need.

Hebrews 4:15–16

He has not dealt with us according to our sins,
    Nor punished us according to our iniquities.
For as the heavens are high above the earth,
    So great is His mercy toward those who fear Him.

Psalm 103:10–11

God, who is rich in mercy, because of His great love with which He loved us, even when we were dead in trespasses, made us alive together with Christ (by grace you have been saved).

Ephesians 2:4–5

Oh, give thanks to the LORD, for He is good!
    For His mercy endures forever.

1 Chronicles 16:34

77

Remember, O Lord, Your tender mercies and Your
  lovingkindnesses,
  For they are from of old.
Do not remember the sins of my youth, nor my
  transgressions;
  According to Your mercy remember me,
  For Your goodness' sake, O Lord.

Psalm 25:6–7

I will hear what God the Lord will speak,
  For He will speak peace
  To His people and to His saints;
  But let them not turn back to folly.
Surely His salvation is near to those who fear Him,
  That glory may dwell in our land.

Mercy and truth have met together;
  Righteousness and peace have kissed.
Truth shall spring out of the earth,
  And righteousness shall look down from heaven.
Yes, the Lord will give what is good;
  And our land will yield its increase.
Righteousness will go before Him,
  And shall make His footsteps our pathway.

Psalm 85:8–13

I will praise You, O LORD, among the peoples,
And I will sing praises to You among the nations.
For Your mercy is great above the heavens,
And Your truth reaches to the clouds.

Be exalted, O God, above the heavens,
And Your glory above all the earth;
That Your beloved may be delivered,
Save with Your right hand, and hear me.

Psalm 108:3–6

Let not mercy and truth forsake you;
Bind them around your neck,
Write them on the tablet of your heart,
And so find favor and high esteem
In the sight of God and man.

Proverbs 3:3–4

His Faithfulness

Let him who thinks he stands take heed lest he fall. No temptation has overtaken you except such as is common to man; but God is faithful, who will not allow you to be tempted beyond what you are able, but with the temptation will also make the way of escape, that you may be able to bear it.

1 Corinthians 10:12–13

I will sing of the mercies of the LORD forever;
With my mouth will I make known Your faithfulness
to all generations.
For I have said, "Mercy shall be built up forever;
Your faithfulness You shall establish in the
very heavens." . . .
O LORD God of hosts,
Who is mighty like You, O LORD?
Your faithfulness also surrounds You.

Psalm 89:1–2, 8

God is faithful, by whom you were called into the fellowship
of His Son, Jesus Christ our Lord.

1 Corinthians 1:9

It is good to give thanks to the LORD,
    And to sing praises to Your name, O Most High;
To declare Your lovingkindness in the morning,
    And Your faithfulness every night.

Psalm 92:1–2

Through the LORD's mercies we are not consumed,
    Because His compassions fail not.
They are new every morning;
    Great is Your faithfulness.

Lamentations 3:22–23

Forever, O LORD,
    Your word is settled in heaven.
Your faithfulness endures to all generations;
    You established the earth, and it abides.
They continue this day according to Your ordinances,
    For all are Your servants.

Psalm 119:89–91

Hear my prayer, O LORD,
   Give ear to my supplications!
   In Your faithfulness answer me,
   And in Your righteousness.
Do not enter into judgment with Your servant,
   For in Your sight no one living is righteous.

Psalm 143:1–2

Your mercy, O LORD, is in the heavens;
   Your faithfulness reaches to the clouds.
Your righteousness is like the great mountains;
   Your judgments are a great deep;
   O LORD, You preserve man and beast.
How precious is Your lovingkindness, O God!
      Therefore the children of men put their trust under
               the shadow of Your wings.

Psalm 36:5–7

His Divine Intervention

If My people who are called by My name will humble themselves, and pray and seek My face, and turn from their wicked ways, then I will hear from heaven, and will forgive their sin and heal their land.

2 Chronicles 7:14

Enter into His gates with thanksgiving,
    And into His courts with praise.
    Be thankful to Him, and bless His name.
For the Lord is good;
    His mercy is everlasting,
    And His truth endures to all generations.

Psalm 100:4–5

Now to Him who is able to do exceedingly abundantly above all that we ask or think, according to the power that works in us, to Him be glory in the church by Christ Jesus to all generations, forever and ever. Amen.

Ephesians 3:20–21

I will rejoice in Jerusalem,
    And joy in My people;
    The voice of weeping shall no longer be heard in her,
    Nor the voice of crying.
No more shall an infant from there live but a few days,
    Nor an old man who has not fulfilled his days;
    For the child shall die one hundred years old,
    But the sinner being one hundred years old shall
            be accursed.
They shall build houses and inhabit them;
    They shall plant vineyards and eat their fruit.
They shall not build and another inhabit;
    They shall not plant and another eat;
    For as the days of a tree, so shall be the days of
            My people,
    And My elect shall long enjoy the work of their hands.
They shall not labor in vain,
    Nor bring forth children for trouble;
    For they shall be the descendants of the blessed of
            the Lord,
    And their offspring with them.
It shall come to pass
    That before they call, I will answer;
    And while they are still speaking, I will hear.

Isaiah 65:19–24

The Spirit also helps in our weaknesses. For we do not know what we should pray for as we ought, but the Spirit Himself makes intercession for us with groanings which cannot be uttered. Now He who searches the hearts knows what the mind of the Spirit is, because He makes intercession for the saints according to the will of God.

Romans 8:26–27

[Jesus], because He continues forever, has an unchangeable priesthood. Therefore He is also able to save to the uttermost those who come to God through Him, since He always lives to make intercession for them.

Hebrews 7:24–25

Grace and peace be multiplied to you in the knowledge of God and of Jesus our Lord, as His divine power has given to us all things that pertain to life and godliness, through the knowledge of Him who called us by glory and virtue, by which have been given to us exceedingly great and precious promises, that through these you may be partakers of the divine nature, having escaped the corruption that is in the world through lust.

2 Peter 1:2–4

His Spirit

When the Helper comes, whom I shall send to you from the Father, the Spirit of truth who proceeds from the Father, He will testify of Me.

John 15:26

Beloved, if God so loved us, we also ought to love one another.

No one has seen God at any time. If we love one another, God abides in us, and His love has been perfected in us. By this we know that we abide in Him, and He in us, because He has given us of His Spirit.

1 John 4:11–13

Do you not know that you are the temple of God and that the Spirit of God dwells in you? If anyone defiles the temple of God, God will destroy him. For the temple of God is holy, which temple you are.

1 Corinthians 3:16–17

God has revealed [His previously hidden wisdom] to us through His Spirit. For the Spirit searches all things, yes, the deep things of God. For what man knows the things of a man except the spirit of the man which is in him? Even so no one knows the things of God except the Spirit of God. Now we have received, not the spirit of the world, but the Spirit who is from God, that we might know the things that have been freely given to us by God.

These things we also speak, not in words which man's wisdom teaches but which the Holy Spirit teaches, comparing spiritual things with spiritual. But the natural man does not receive the things of the Spirit of God, for they are foolishness to him; nor can he know them, because they are spiritually discerned. But he who is spiritual judges all things, yet he himself is rightly judged by no one. For "who has known the mind of the Lord that he may instruct Him?" But we have the mind of Christ.

1 Corinthians 2:10–16

Do you not know that your body is the temple of the Holy Spirit who is in you, whom you have from God, and you are not your own? For you were bought at a price; therefore glorify God in your body and in your spirit, which are God's.

1 Corinthians 6:19–20

If you love Me, keep My commandments. And I will pray the Father, and He will give you another Helper, that He may abide with you forever—the Spirit of truth, whom the world cannot receive, because it neither sees Him nor knows Him; but you know Him, for He dwells with you and will be in you.

John 14:15–17

Having believed [in the gospel of your salvation], you were sealed with the Holy Spirit of promise, who is the guarantee of our inheritance until the redemption of the purchased possession, to the praise of His glory.

Ephesians 1:13–14

Let no corrupt word proceed out of your mouth, but what is good for necessary edification, that it may impart grace to the hearers. And do not grieve the Holy Spirit of God, by whom you were sealed for the day of redemption. Let all bitterness, wrath, anger, clamor, and evil speaking be put away from you, with all malice. And be kind to one another, tenderhearted, forgiving one another, even as God in Christ forgave you.

Ephesians 4:29–32

His Strength

The Lord is my strength and my shield;
    My heart trusted in Him, and I am helped;
    Therefore my heart greatly rejoices,
    And with my song I will praise Him.
The Lord is their strength,
    And He is the saving refuge of His anointed.
Save Your people,
    And bless Your inheritance;
    Shepherd them also,
    And bear them up forever.

Psalm 28:7–9

The Lord is my light and my salvation;
    Whom shall I fear?
    The Lord is the strength of my life;
    Of whom shall I be afraid?
When the wicked came against me
    To eat up my flesh,
    My enemies and foes,
    They stumbled and fell.

Psalm 27:1–2

God is our refuge and strength,
A very present help in trouble.
Therefore we will not fear,
Even though the earth be removed,
And though the mountains be carried into the midst
of the sea;
Though its waters roar and be troubled,
Though the mountains shake with its swelling. Selah
There is a river whose streams shall make glad the city
of God,
The holy place of the tabernacle of the Most High.
God is in the midst of her, she shall not be moved;
God shall help her, just at the break of dawn.

Psalm 46:1–5

The salvation of the righteous is from the LORD;
He is their strength in the time of trouble.
And the LORD shall help them and deliver them;
He shall deliver them from the wicked,
And save them,
Because they trust in Him.

Psalm 37:39–40

I can do all things through Christ who strengthens me.

Philippians 4:13

O God, You are more awesome than Your holy places.
    The God of Israel is He who gives strength and power
            to His people.
    Blessed be God!

Psalm 68:35

Give unto the LORD, O you mighty ones,
    Give unto the LORD glory and strength.
Give unto the LORD the glory due to His name;
    Worship the LORD in the beauty of holiness.
The voice of the LORD is over the waters;
    The God of glory thunders;
    The LORD is over many waters.
The voice of the LORD is powerful;
    The voice of the LORD is full of majesty. . . .
The voice of the LORD makes the deer give birth,
    And strips the forests bare;
    And in His temple everyone says, "Glory!"
The LORD sat enthroned at the Flood,
    And the LORD sits as King forever.
The LORD will give strength to His people;
    The LORD will bless His people with peace.

Psalm 29:1–4, 9–11

His Rest

Come to Me, all you who labor and are heavy laden, and I will give you rest. Take My yoke upon you and learn from Me, for I am gentle and lowly in heart, and you will find rest for your souls. For My yoke is easy and My burden is light.

Matthew 11:28–30

There remains . . . a rest for the people of God. For he who has entered His rest has himself also ceased from his works as God did from His. Let us therefore be diligent to enter that rest, lest anyone fall according to the same example of disobedience.

Hebrews 4:9–11

Commit your way to the LORD,
Trust also in Him,
And He shall bring it to pass.
    He shall bring forth your righteousness as the light,
And your justice as the noonday.
    Rest in the LORD, and wait patiently for Him.

Psalm 37:5–7

God raised up [Jesus of Nazareth], having loosed the pains of death, because it was not possible that He should be held by it. For David says concerning Him:

"I foresaw the LORD always before my face,
For He is at my right hand, that I may not be shaken.
Therefore my heart rejoiced, and my tongue was glad;
Moreover my flesh also will rest in hope.
For You will not leave my soul in Hades,
Nor will You allow Your Holy One to see corruption."

Acts 2:24–27

The LORD preserves the simple;
I was brought low, and He saved me.
Return to your rest, O my soul,
For the LORD has dealt bountifully with you.

Psalm 116:6–7

Thus says the LORD:

"Stand in the ways and see,
And ask for the old paths, where the good way is,
And walk in it;
Then you will find rest for your souls."

Jeremiah 6:16

[The Lord] said, "My Presence will go with you, and I will give you rest."

Exodus 33:14

The Sabbath was made for man, and not man for the Sabbath.

Mark 2:27

🍂 Fruitfulness 🍂

The fruit of the Spirit is love, joy, peace, longsuffering, kindness, goodness, faithfulness, gentleness, self-control. Against such there is no law. And those who are Christ's have crucified the flesh with its passions and desires. If we live in the Spirit, let us also walk in the Spirit. Let us not become conceited, provoking one another, envying one another.

Galatians 5:22–26

[We] do not cease to pray for you, and to ask that you may be filled with the knowledge of His will in all wisdom and spiritual understanding; that you may walk worthy of the Lord, fully pleasing Him, being fruitful in every good work and increasing in the knowledge of God; strengthened with all might, according to His glorious power, for all patience and longsuffering with joy; giving thanks to the Father who has qualified us to be partakers of the inheritance of the saints in the light. He has delivered us from the power of darkness and conveyed us into the kingdom of the Son of His love.

Colossians 1:9–13

I am the true vine, and My Father is the vinedresser. Every branch in Me that does not bear fruit He takes away; and every branch that bears fruit He prunes, that it may bear more fruit. You are already clean because of the word which I have spoken to you. Abide in Me, and I in you. As the branch cannot bear fruit of itself, unless it abides in the vine, neither can you, unless you abide in Me.

I am the vine, you are the branches. He who abides in Me, and I in him, bears much fruit; for without Me you can do nothing. If anyone does not abide in Me, he is cast out as a branch and is withered; and they gather them and throw them into the fire, and they are burned. If you abide in Me, and My words abide in you, you will ask what you desire, and it shall be done for you. By this My Father is glorified, that you bear much fruit; so you will be My disciples.

As the Father loved Me, I also have loved you; abide in My love.

John 15:1–9

My fruit is better than gold, yes, than fine gold,
　And my revenue than choice silver.
I traverse the way of righteousness,
　In the midst of the paths of justice,
That I may cause those who love me to inherit wealth,
　That I may fill their treasuries.

Proverbs 8:19–21

Blessed is every one who fears the LORD,
     Who walks in His ways.
When you eat the labor of your hands,
     You shall be happy, and it shall be well with you.
Your wife shall be like a fruitful vine
     In the very heart of your house,
     Your children like olive plants
     All around your table.
Behold, thus shall the man be blessed
     Who fears the LORD.

Psalm 128:1–4

Hope

I consider that the sufferings of this present time are not worthy to be compared with the glory which shall be revealed in us. For the earnest expectation of the creation eagerly waits for the revealing of the sons of God.... For we were saved in this hope [of adoption and the redemption of our body], but hope that is seen is not hope; for why does one still hope for what he sees? But if we hope for what we do not see, we eagerly wait for it with perseverance.

Romans 8:18–19, 24–25

Behold, the eye of the LORD is on those who fear Him,
    On those who hope in His mercy,
To deliver their soul from death,
    And to keep them alive in famine.
Our soul waits for the LORD;
    He is our help and our shield.
For our heart shall rejoice in Him,
    Because we have trusted in His holy name.
Let Your mercy, O LORD, be upon us,
    Just as we hope in You.

Psalm 33:18–22

Through the LORD's mercies we are not consumed,
Because His compassions fail not.
They are new every morning;
Great is Your faithfulness.
"The LORD is my portion," says my soul,
"Therefore I hope in Him!"

Lamentations 3:22–24

I, therefore, the prisoner of the Lord, beseech you to walk worthy of the calling with which you were called, with all lowliness and gentleness, with longsuffering, bearing with one another in love, endeavoring to keep the unity of the Spirit in the bond of peace. There is one body and one Spirit, just as you were called in one hope of your calling.

Ephesians 4:1–4

We should live soberly, righteously, and godly in the present age, looking for the blessed hope and glorious appearing of our great God and Savior Jesus Christ, who gave Himself for us, that He might redeem us from every lawless deed and purify for Himself His own special people, zealous for good works.

Titus 2:12–14

May the God of hope fill you with all joy and peace in believing, that you may abound in hope by the power of the Holy Spirit.

Romans 15:13

I became a minister . . . to fulfill the word of God, the mystery which has been hidden from ages and from generations, but now has been revealed to His saints. To them God willed to make known what are the riches of the glory of this mystery among the Gentiles: which is Christ in you, the hope of glory.

Colossians 1:25–27

We . . . glory in tribulations, knowing that tribulation produces perseverance; and perseverance, character; and character, hope. Now hope does not disappoint, because the love of God has been poured out in our hearts by the Holy Spirit who was given to us.

Romans 5:3–5

Abundance

For the LORD God is a sun and shield;
    The LORD will give grace and glory;
    No good thing will He withhold
    From those who walk uprightly.
O LORD of hosts,
    Blessed is the man who trusts in You!

Psalm 84:11–12

God is able to make all grace abound toward you, that you, always having all sufficiency in all things, may have an abundance for every good work.

2 Corinthians 9:8

Blessed be the God and Father of our Lord Jesus Christ, who according to His abundant mercy has begotten us again to a living hope through the resurrection of Jesus Christ from the dead, to an inheritance incorruptible and undefiled and that does not fade away, reserved in heaven for you, who are kept by the power of God through faith for salvation ready to be revealed in the last time.

1 Peter 1:3–5

O Israel, hope in the LORD;
    For with the LORD there is mercy,
    And with Him is abundant redemption.
And He shall redeem Israel
    From all his iniquities.

Psalm 130:7–8

God, determining to show more abundantly to the heirs of promise the immutability of His counsel, confirmed it by an oath, that . . . we might have strong consolation, who have fled for refuge to lay hold of the hope set before us.

Hebrews 6:17–18

The grace of our Lord was exceedingly abundant, with faith and love which are in Christ Jesus. This is a faithful saying and worthy of all acceptance, that Christ Jesus came into the world to save sinners, of whom I am chief. However, for this reason I obtained mercy, that in me first Jesus Christ might show all longsuffering, as a pattern to those who are going to believe on Him for everlasting life.

1 Timothy 1:14–16

Rejoice the soul of Your servant,
  For to You, O Lord, I lift up my soul.
For You, Lord, are good, and ready to forgive,
  And abundant in mercy to all those who call upon You.
                                                    Psalm 86:4–5

[God] is able to do exceedingly abundantly above all that
we ask or think, according to the power that works in us.
                                                    Ephesians 3:20

God's
Truth

Your Heavenly Father

I will be a Father to you,
And you shall be My sons and daughters,
Says the LORD Almighty.

2 Corinthians 6:18

You, O LORD, are our Father;
Our Redeemer from Everlasting is Your name.

Isaiah 63:16

As a father pities his children,
So the LORD pities those who fear Him.

Psalm 103:13

We have known and believed the love that God has for us. God is love, and he who abides in love abides in God, and God in him.

1 John 4:16

Let your conduct be without covetousness; be content with such things as you have. For [Jesus] Himself has said, "I will never leave you nor forsake you."

Hebrews 13:5

Behold what manner of love the Father has bestowed on us, that we should be called children of God!

1 John 3:1

Not everyone who says to Me, "Lord, Lord," shall enter the kingdom of heaven, but he who does the will of My Father in heaven.

Matthew 7:21

Whoever does the will of My Father in heaven is My brother and sister and mother.

Matthew 12:50

Blessed be the God and Father of our Lord Jesus Christ, who has blessed us with every spiritual blessing in the heavenly places in Christ, just as He chose us in Him before the foundation of the world, that we should be holy and without blame before Him in love, having predestined us to adoption as sons by Jesus Christ to Himself, according to the good pleasure of His will.

Ephesians 1:3–5

You received the Spirit of adoption by whom we cry out, "Abba, Father." The Spirit Himself bears witness with our spirit that we are children of God.

Romans 8:15–16

❧ Jesus: Your Savior ❧

For God so loved the world that He gave His only begotten Son, that whoever believes in Him should not perish but have everlasting life. For God did not send His Son into the world to condemn the world, but that the world through Him might be saved.

John 3:16–7

God demonstrates His own love toward us, in that while we were still sinners, Christ died for us.

Romans 5:8

He who believes in the Son has everlasting life; and he who does not believe the Son shall not see life, but the wrath of God abides on him.

John 3:36

As many as received [Jesus], to them He gave the right to become children of God, to those who believe in His name.

John 1:12

By grace you have been saved through faith, and that not of yourselves; it is the gift of God, not of works, lest anyone should boast.

Ephesians 2:8–9

Behold, I stand at the door and knock. If anyone hears My voice and opens the door, I will come in to him and dine with him, and he with Me.

Revelation 3:20

"The word is near you, in your mouth and in your heart" (that is, the word of faith which we preach): that if you confess with your mouth the Lord Jesus and believe in your heart that God has raised Him from the dead, you will be saved. For with the heart one believes unto righteousness, and with the mouth confession is made unto salvation.

Romans 10:8–10

God has given us eternal life, and this life is in His Son. He who has the Son has life; he who does not have the Son of God does not have life. These things I have written to you who believe in the name of the Son of God, that you may know that you have eternal life, and that you may continue to believe in the name of the Son of God.

1 John 5:11–13

The Holy Spirit: Your Helper

When He, the Spirit of truth, has come, He will guide you into all truth; for He will not speak on His own authority, but whatever He hears He will speak; and He will tell you things to come.

John 16:13

These things I have spoken to you while being present with you. But the Helper, the Holy Spirit, whom the Father will send in My name, He will teach you all things, and bring to your remembrance all things that I said to you.

John 14:25–26

Anyone who speaks a word against the Son of Man, it will be forgiven him; but to him who blasphemes against the Holy Spirit, it will not be forgiven.

Now when they bring you to the synagogues and magistrates and authorities, do not worry about how or what you should answer, or what you should say. For the Holy Spirit will teach you in that very hour what you ought to say.

Luke 12:10–12

Jesus said to [His disciples] again, "Peace to you! As the Father has sent Me, I also send you." And when He had said this, He breathed on them, and said to them, "Receive the Holy Spirit. If you forgive the sins of any, they are forgiven them; if you retain the sins of any, they are retained."

John 20:21–23

You shall receive power when the Holy Spirit has come upon you; and you shall be witnesses to Me in Jerusalem, and in all Judea and Samaria, and to the end of the earth.

Acts 1:8

It is the Spirit who gives life; the flesh profits nothing. The words that I speak to you are spirit, and they are life.

John 6:63

In [Christ] you also trusted, after you heard the word of truth, the gospel of your salvation; in whom also, having believed, you were sealed with the Holy Spirit of promise, who is the guarantee of our inheritance until the redemption of the purchased possession, to the praise of His glory.

Ephesians 1:13–14

 His Word

The word of God is living and powerful, and sharper than any two-edged sword, piercing even to the division of soul and spirit, and of joints and marrow, and is a discerner of the thoughts and intents of the heart. And there is no creature hidden from His sight, but all things are naked and open to the eyes of Him to whom we must give account.

Hebrews 4:12–13

Your word I have hidden in my heart,
That I might not sin against You.
Blessed are You, O LORD!
Teach me Your statutes. . . .
I will delight myself in Your statutes;
I will not forget Your word.

Psalm 119:11–12, 16

By the word of the LORD the heavens were made,
And all the host of them by the breath of His mouth.
He gathers the waters of the sea together as a heap;
He lays up the deep in storehouses.

Psalm 33:6–7

How sweet are Your words to my taste,
    Sweeter than honey to my mouth!
Through Your precepts I get understanding;
    Therefore I hate every false way.
Your word is a lamp to my feet
    And a light to my path.

Psalm 119:103–105

In the beginning was the Word, and the Word was with God, and the Word was God. He was in the beginning with God. All things were made through Him, and without Him nothing was made that was made. In Him was life, and the life was the light of men.

John 1:1–4

As newborn babes, desire the pure milk of the word, that you may grow thereby, if indeed you have tasted that the Lord is gracious.

1 Peter 2:2–3

Heaven and earth will pass away, but My words will by no means pass away.

Luke 21:33

The grass withers, the flower fades,
But the word of our God stands forever.

Isaiah 40:8

Jesus said to those Jews who believed Him, "If you abide in My word, you are My disciples indeed. And you shall know the truth, and the truth shall make you free."

John 8:31–32

Heaven: Your Home

This is the will of the Father who sent Me, that of all He has given Me I should lose nothing, but should raise it up at the last day. And this is the will of Him who sent Me, that everyone who sees the Son and believes in Him may have everlasting life; and I will raise him up at the last day.

John 6:39–40

"God will wipe away every tear from their eyes; there shall be no more death, nor sorrow, nor crying. There shall be no more pain, for the former things have passed away."

Then He who sat on the throne said, "Behold, I make all things new." And He said to me, "Write, for these words are true and faithful."

And He said to me, "It is done! I am the Alpha and the Omega, the Beginning and the End. I will give of the fountain of the water of life freely to him who thirsts."

Revelation 21:4–6

Our citizenship is in heaven, from which we also eagerly wait for the Savior, the Lord Jesus Christ, who will transform our lowly body that it may be conformed to His glorious body, according to the working by which He is able even to subdue all things to Himself.

Philippians 3:20–21

We give thanks to the God and Father of our Lord Jesus Christ . . . because of the hope which is laid up for you in heaven, of which you heard before in the word of the truth of the gospel, which has come to you, as it has also in all the world, and is bringing forth fruit, as it is also among you since the day you heard and knew the grace of God in truth.

Colossians 1:3, 5–6

[Jesus] took the cup, and when He had given thanks He gave it to them, and they all drank from it. And He said to them, "This is My blood of the new covenant, which is shed for many. Assuredly, I say to you, I will no longer drink of the fruit of the vine until that day when I drink it new in the kingdom of God."

Mark 14:23–25

Surely goodness and mercy shall follow me
    All the days of my life;
    And I will dwell in the house of the LORD
    Forever.

Psalm 23:6

In [Jesus Christ] we have redemption through His blood, the forgiveness of sins, according to the riches of His grace which He made to abound toward us in all wisdom and prudence, having made known to us the mystery of His will, according to His good pleasure which He purposed in Himself, that in the dispensation of the fullness of the times He might gather together in one all things in Christ, both which are in heaven and which are on earth—in Him. In Him also we have obtained an inheritance, being predestined according to the purpose of Him who works all things according to the counsel of His will, that we who first trusted in Christ should be to the praise of His glory.

Ephesians 1:7–12

Christ's Return

We who are alive and remain until the coming of the Lord will by no means precede those who are asleep. For the Lord Himself will descend from heaven with a shout, with the voice of an archangel, and with the trumpet of God. And the dead in Christ will rise first. Then we who are alive and remain shall be caught up together with them in the clouds to meet the Lord in the air. And thus we shall always be with the Lord. Therefore comfort one another with these words.

1 Thessalonians 4:15–18

There will be signs in the sun, in the moon, and in the stars; and on the earth distress of nations, with perplexity, the sea and the waves roaring; men's hearts failing them from fear and the expectation of those things which are coming on the earth, for the powers of the heavens will be shaken. Then they will see the Son of Man coming in a cloud with power and great glory. Now when these things begin to happen, look up and lift up your heads, because your redemption draws near.

Luke 21:25–28

Beloved, now we are children of God; and it has not yet been revealed what we shall be, but we know that when He is revealed, we shall be like Him, for we shall see Him as He is. And everyone who has this hope in Him purifies himself, just as He is pure.

1 John 3:2–3

Let not your heart be troubled; you believe in God, believe also in Me. In My Father's house are many mansions; if it were not so, I would have told you. I go to prepare a place for you. And if I go and prepare a place for you, I will come again and receive you to Myself; that where I am, there you may be also. And where I go you know, and the way you know.

John 14:1–4

We should live soberly, righteously, and godly in the present age, looking for the blessed hope and glorious appearing of our great God and Savior Jesus Christ, who gave Himself for us, that He might redeem us from every lawless deed and purify for Himself His own special people, zealous for good works.

Titus 2:12–14

There is laid up for me the crown of righteousness, which the Lord, the righteous Judge, will give to me on that Day, and not to me only but also to all who have loved His appearing.

2 Timothy 4:8

While they looked steadfastly toward heaven as He went up, behold, two men stood by them in white apparel, who also said, "Men of Galilee, why do you stand gazing up into heaven? This same Jesus, who was taken up from you into heaven, will so come in like manner as you saw Him go into heaven."

Acts 1:10–11

Heavenly Rewards

As it is written:
"Eye has not seen, nor ear heard,
Nor have entered into the heart of man
The things which God has prepared for those who
love Him."

1 Corinthians 2:9

Violence shall no longer be heard in your land,
Neither wasting nor destruction within your borders;
But you shall call your walls Salvation,
And your gates Praise.
The sun shall no longer be your light by day,
Nor for brightness shall the moon give light to you;
But the LORD will be to you an everlasting light,
And your God your glory.
Your sun shall no longer go down,
Nor shall your moon withdraw itself;
For the LORD will be your everlasting light,
And the days of your mourning shall be ended.

Isaiah 60:18–20

Many of those who sleep in the dust of the earth shall awake,
    Some to everlasting life,
    Some to shame and everlasting contempt.
Those who are wise shall shine
    Like the brightness of the firmament,
    And those who turn many to righteousness
    Like the stars forever and ever.

Daniel 12:2–3

Since the beginning of the world
    Men have not heard nor perceived by the ear,
    Nor has the eye seen any God besides You,
    Who acts for the one who waits for Him.
You meet him who rejoices and does righteousness,
    Who remembers You in Your ways.

Isaiah 64:4–5

"Behold, I am coming quickly, and My reward is with Me, to give to every one according to his work. I am the Alpha and the Omega, the Beginning and the End, the First and the Last."

Blessed are those who do His commandments, that they may have the right to the tree of life, and may enter through the gates into the city.

Revelation 22:12–14

The wicked man does deceptive work,
But he who sows righteousness will have a sure reward.

Proverbs 11:18

Take heed that you do not do your charitable deeds before men, to be seen by them. Otherwise you have no reward from your Father in heaven.

Matthew 6:1

God will bring every work into judgment,
Including every secret thing,
Whether good or evil.

Ecclesiastes 12:14

Turning Back to God

Let the wicked forsake his way,
    And the unrighteous man his thoughts;
    Let him return to the Lord,
    And He will have mercy on him;
    And to our God,
    For He will abundantly pardon.

Isaiah 55:7

If anyone cleanses himself from [dishonor], he will be a vessel for honor, sanctified and useful for the Master, prepared for every good work.

2 Timothy 2:21

Submit to God. Resist the devil and he will flee from you. Draw near to God and He will draw near to you. Cleanse your hands, you sinners; and purify your hearts, you double-minded. Lament and mourn and weep! Let your laughter be turned to mourning and your joy to gloom. Humble yourselves in the sight of the Lord, and He will lift you up.

James 4:7–10

Now by this we know that we know [Jesus], if we keep His commandments. He who says, "I know Him," and does not keep His commandments, is a liar, and the truth is not in him. But whoever keeps His word, truly the love of God is perfected in him. By this we know that we are in Him. He who says he abides in Him ought himself also to walk just as He walked.

1 John 2:3–6

Laying aside all malice, all deceit, hypocrisy, envy, and all evil speaking, as newborn babes, desire the pure milk of the word, that you may grow thereby, if indeed you have tasted that the Lord is gracious.

1 Peter 2:1–3

Be doers of the word, and not hearers only, deceiving yourselves. For if anyone is a hearer of the word and not a doer, he is like a man observing his natural face in a mirror; for he observes himself, goes away, and immediately forgets what kind of man he was. But he who looks into the perfect law of liberty and continues in it, and is not a forgetful hearer but a doer of the work, this one will be blessed in what he does.

James 1:22–25

In Him we live and move and have our being, as also some of your own poets have said, "For we are also His offspring."

Acts 17:28

The Lord has appeared of old to me, saying:
    "Yes, I have loved you with an everlasting love;
    Therefore with lovingkindness I have drawn you."

Jeremiah 31:3

Prayer

Be anxious for nothing, but in everything by prayer and supplication, with thanksgiving, let your requests be made known to God; and the peace of God, which surpasses all understanding, will guard your hearts and minds through Christ Jesus.

Philippians 4:6–7

Assuredly, I say to you, whatever you bind on earth will be bound in heaven, and whatever you loose on earth will be loosed in heaven. Again I say to you that if two of you agree on earth concerning anything that they ask, it will be done for them by My Father in heaven.

Matthew 18:18–19

Confess your trespasses to one another, and pray for one another, that you may be healed. The effective, fervent prayer of a righteous man avails much.

James 5:16

LORD, I cry out to You;
   Make haste to me!
   Give ear to my voice when I cry out to You.
Let my prayer be set before You as incense,
   The lifting up of my hands as the evening sacrifice.

Psalm 141:1–2

"I say to you, ask, and it will be given to you; seek, and you will find; knock, and it will be opened to you. For everyone who asks receives, and he who seeks finds, and to him who knocks it will be opened.

Luke 11:9–10

For the eyes of the LORD are on the righteous,
   And His ears are open to their prayers;
   But the face of the LORD is against those who do evil.

1 Peter 3:12

Seeing then that we have a great High Priest who has passed through the heavens, Jesus the Son of God, let us hold fast our confession. For we do not have a High Priest who cannot sympathize with our weaknesses, but was in all points tempted as we are, yet without sin. Let us therefore come boldly to the throne of grace, that we may obtain mercy and find grace to help in time of need.

Hebrews 4:14–16

Call to Me, and I will answer you, and show you great and mighty things, which you do not know.

Jeremiah 33:3

What man is there among you who, if his son asks for bread, will give him a stone? Or if he asks for a fish, will he give him a serpent? If you then, being evil, know how to give good gifts to your children, how much more will your Father who is in heaven give good things to those who ask Him!

Matthew 7:9–11

❧ Healing ❧

Bless the LORD, O my soul,
    And forget not all His benefits:
Who forgives all your iniquities,
    Who heals all your diseases.

Psalm 103:2–3

We do not lose heart. Even though our outward man is perishing, yet the inward man is being renewed day by day. For our light affliction, which is but for a moment, is working for us a far more exceeding and eternal weight of glory.

2 Corinthians 4:16–17

The righteous cry out, and the LORD hears,
    And delivers them out of all their troubles.
The LORD is near to those who have a broken heart,
    And saves such as have a contrite spirit.
Many are the afflictions of the righteous,
    But the LORD delivers him out of them all.

Psalm 34:17–19

The LORD God is my strength;
    He will make my feet like deer's feet,
    And He will make me walk on my high hills.

Habakkuk 3:19

[Christ] Himself bore our sins in His own body on the tree, that we, having died to sins, might live for righteousness— by whose stripes you were healed.

1 Peter 2:24

My flesh and my heart fail;
    But God is the strength of my heart and my
                portion forever.

Psalm 73:26

"To you who fear My name
    The Sun of Righteousness shall arise
    With healing in His wings;
    And you shall go out
    And grow fat like stall-fed calves.
You shall trample the wicked,
    For they shall be ashes under the soles of your feet
    On the day that I do this,"
    Says the LORD of hosts.

Malachi 4:2–3

Is this not the fast that I have chosen:
    To loose the bonds of wickedness,
    To undo the heavy burdens,
    To let the oppressed go free,
    And that you break every yoke?
Is it not to share your bread with the hungry,
    And that you bring to your house the poor who are
            cast out;
    When you see the naked, that you cover him,
    And not hide yourself from your own flesh?
Then your light shall break forth like the morning,
    Your healing shall spring forth speedily,
    And your righteousness shall go before you;
    The glory of the LORD shall be your rear guard.
Then you shall call, and the Lord will answer;
    You shall cry, and He will say, "Here I am."

Isaiah 58:6–9

Is anyone among you sick? Let him call for the elders of the
church, and let them pray over him, anointing him with oil
in the name of the Lord. And the prayer of faith will save
the sick, and the Lord will raise him up.

James 5:14

God's
Solutions

When There Is Anger

Let every man be swift to hear, slow to speak, slow to wrath; for the wrath of man does not produce the righteousness of God.

Therefore lay aside all filthiness and overflow of wickedness, and receive with meekness the implanted word, which is able to save your souls.

James 1:19–21

A soft answer turns away wrath,
But a harsh word stirs up anger.
The tongue of the wise uses knowledge rightly,
But the mouth of fools pours forth foolishness.

Proverbs 15:1–2

The wisdom that is from above is first pure, then peaceable, gentle, willing to yield, full of mercy and good fruits, without partiality and without hypocrisy. Now the fruit of righteousness is sown in peace by those who make peace.

James 3:17–18

Cease from anger, and forsake wrath;
    Do not fret—it only causes harm.
For evildoers shall be cut off;
    But those who wait on the LORD,
    They shall inherit the earth.

Psalm 37:8–9

He who is slow to anger is better than the mighty,
    And he who rules his spirit than he who takes a city.

Proverbs 16:32

The LORD is merciful and gracious,
    Slow to anger, and abounding in mercy.
He will not always strive with us,
    Nor will He keep His anger forever.
He has not dealt with us according to our sins,
    Nor punished us according to our iniquities.
For as the heavens are high above the earth,
    So great is His mercy toward those who fear Him.

Psalm 103:8–11

"Be angry, and do not sin": do not let the sun go down on
your wrath, nor give place to the devil.

Ephesians 4:26–27

When There Is Disappointment

My heart was grieved,
   And I was vexed in my mind.
I was so foolish and ignorant;
   I was like a beast before You.
Nevertheless I am continually with You;
   You hold me by my right hand.
You will guide me with Your counsel,
   And afterward receive me to glory.

Psalm 73:21–24

God is not the author of confusion but of peace.

1 Corinthians 14:33

Create in me a clean heart, O God,
   And renew a steadfast spirit within me.
Do not cast me away from Your presence,
   And do not take Your Holy Spirit from me.
Restore to me the joy of Your salvation,
   And uphold me by Your generous Spirit.

Psalm 51:10–12

For He is our God,
　　And we are the people of His pasture,
　　And the sheep of His hand.

Psalm 95:7

Wait on the LORD;
　　Be of good courage,
　　And He shall strengthen your heart;
　　Wait, I say, on the LORD!

Psalm 27:14

The LORD also will be a refuge for the oppressed,
　　A refuge in times of trouble.
And those who know Your name will put their trust
　　　　　　in You;
　　For You, LORD, have not forsaken those who seek You.

Psalm 9:9–10

Who shall separate us from the love of Christ? Shall tribulation, or distress, or persecution, or famine, or nakedness, or peril, or sword? As it is written:

　　"For Your sake we are killed all day long;
　　We are accounted as sheep for the slaughter."

　　Yet in all these things we are more than conquerors through Him who loved us.

Romans 8:35–37

The Spirit of the Lord God is upon Me,
　　Because the Lord has anointed Me
　　To preach good tidings to the poor;
　　He has sent Me to heal the brokenhearted,
　　To proclaim liberty to the captives,
　　And the opening of the prison to those who are bound;
To proclaim the acceptable year of the Lord,
　　And the day of vengeance of our God;
　　To comfort all who mourn,
To console those who mourn in Zion,
　　To give them beauty for ashes,
　　The oil of joy for mourning,
　　The garment of praise for the spirit of heaviness;
　　That they may be called trees of righteousness,
　　The planting of the Lord, that He may be glorified.

Isaiah 61:1–3

When There Is Failure

Now may our Lord Jesus Christ Himself, and our God and Father, who has loved us and given us everlasting consolation and good hope by grace, comfort your hearts and establish you in every good word and work.

2 Thessalonians 2:16–17

I will bring the blind by a way they did not know;
    I will lead them in paths they have not known.
    I will make darkness light before them,
    And crooked places straight.
    These things I will do for them,
    And not forsake them.

Isaiah 42:16

Why are you cast down, O my soul?
    And why are you disquieted within me?
    Hope in God;
    For I shall yet praise Him,
    The help of my countenance and my God.

Psalm 42:11

I, the LORD your God, will hold your right hand,
　　Saying to you, "Fear not, I will help you."

I will be glad and rejoice in Your mercy,
　　For You have considered my trouble;
　　You have known my soul in adversities.

Psalm 31:7

Will the Lord cast off forever?
　　And will He be favorable no more?
Has His mercy ceased forever?
　　Has His promise failed forevermore?
Has God forgotten to be gracious?
　　Has He in anger shut up His tender mercies? . . .
I will remember the works of the Lord;
　　Surely I will remember Your wonders of old.
I will also meditate on all Your work,
　　And talk of Your deeds.
Your way, O God, is in the sanctuary;
　　Who is so great a God as our God?

Psalm 77:7–9, 11–13

The LORD is good,
A stronghold in the day of trouble;
And He knows those who trust in Him.

Nahum 1:7

I have loved you with an everlasting love;
Therefore with lovingkindness I have drawn you.
Again I will build you, and you shall be rebuilt,
O virgin of Israel!
You shall again be adorned with your tambourines,
And shall go forth in the dances of those who rejoice.

Jeremiah 31:3–4

We know that all things work together for good to those
who love God, to those who are the called according to His
purpose. For whom He foreknew, He also predestined to
be conformed to the image of His Son.

Romans 8:28–29

I know that my Redeemer lives,
And He shall stand at last on the earth;
And after my skin is destroyed, this I know,
That in my flesh I shall see God.

Job 19:25–26

When There Is Financial Trouble

The love of money is a root of all kinds of evil, for which some have strayed from the faith in their greediness, and pierced themselves through with many sorrows.

But you, O man of God, flee these things and pursue righteousness, godliness, faith, love, patience, gentleness.

1 Timothy 6:10–11

Command those who are rich in this present age not to be haughty, nor to trust in uncertain riches but in the living God, who gives us richly all things to enjoy. Let them do good, that they be rich in good works, ready to give, willing to share, storing up for themselves a good foundation for the time to come, that they may lay hold on eternal life.

1 Timothy 6:17–19

My God shall supply all your need according to His riches in glory by Christ Jesus.

Philippians 4:19

Remove falsehood and lies far from me;
>   Give me neither poverty nor riches—
>   Feed me with the food allotted to me;
Lest I be full and deny You,
>   And say, "Who is the Lord?"
>   Or lest I be poor and steal,
>   And profane the name of my God.

Proverbs 30:8–9

He who trusts in his riches will fall,
>   But the righteous will flourish like foliage.
He who troubles his own house will inherit the wind,
>   And the fool will be servant to the wise of heart.
The fruit of the righteous is a tree of life,
>   And he who wins souls is wise.

Proverbs 11:28–30

Trust in the Lord, and do good;
>   Dwell in the land, and feed on His faithfulness.
Delight yourself also in the Lord,
>   And He shall give you the desires of your heart.

Psalm 37:3–4

The young lions lack and suffer hunger;
    But those who seek the Lord shall not lack any
        good thing.

Psalm 34:10

There is one who makes himself rich, yet has nothing;
    And one who makes himself poor, yet has great
        riches. . . .
Wealth gained by dishonesty will be diminished,
    But he who gathers by labor will increase.

Proverbs 13:7, 11

When There Is Heartbreak

The Spirit of the Lord God is upon Me,
 Because the Lord has anointed Me
 To preach good tidings to the poor;
 He has sent Me to heal the brokenhearted,
 To proclaim liberty to the captives,
 And the opening of the prison to those who are bound;
To proclaim the acceptable year of the Lord,
 And the day of vengeance of our God;
 To comfort all who mourn.

Isaiah 61:1–2

You are the helper of the fatherless.

Psalm 10:14

Those who sow in tears
 Shall reap in joy.
He who continually goes forth weeping,
 Bearing seed for sowing,
 Shall doubtless come again with rejoicing,
 Bringing his sheaves with him.

Psalm 126:5–6

Cast your burden on the Lord,
    And He shall sustain you;
    He shall never permit the righteous to be moved.

Psalm 55:22

I say to you who hear: Love your enemies, do good to those who hate you, bless those who curse you, and pray for those who spitefully use you.

Luke 6:27–28

For the Lord God will help Me;
    Therefore I will not be disgraced;
    Therefore I have set My face like a flint,
    And I know that I will not be ashamed.

Isaiah 50:7

The Lord also will be a refuge for the oppressed,
    A refuge in times of trouble.
Those who know Your name will put their trust in You;
    For You, Lord, have not forsaken those who seek You.

Psalm 9:9–10

Blessed be the God and Father of our Lord Jesus Christ, the Father of mercies and God of all comfort, who comforts us in all our tribulation, that we may be able to comfort those who are in any trouble, with the comfort with which we ourselves are comforted by God. For as the sufferings of Christ abound in us, so our consolation also abounds through Christ.

2 Corinthians 1:3–5

❧ When There Is Sexual Impurity ❧

Most assuredly, I say to you, whoever commits sin is a slave of sin. And a slave does not abide in the house forever, but a son abides forever. Therefore if the Son makes you free, you shall be free indeed.

John 8:34–36

No temptation has overtaken you except such as is common to man; but God is faithful, who will not allow you to be tempted beyond what you are able, but with the temptation will also make the way of escape, that you may be able to bear it.

1 Corinthians 10:13

Walk in the Spirit, and you shall not fulfill the lust of the flesh. For the flesh lusts against the Spirit, and the Spirit against the flesh; and these are contrary to one another, so that you do not do the things that you wish. But if you are led by the Spirit, you are not under the law.

Galatians 5:16–18

If anyone is in Christ, he is a new creation; old things have passed away; behold, all things have become new.

2 Corinthians 5:17

The Lord knows how to deliver the godly out of temptations and to reserve the unjust under punishment for the day of judgment.

2 Peter 2:9

Do you not know that your bodies are members of Christ? Shall I then take the members of Christ and make them members of a harlot? Certainly not! Or do you not know that he who is joined to a harlot is one body with her? For "the two," [Christ] says, "shall become one flesh." But he who is joined to the Lord is one spirit with Him.

Flee sexual immorality. Every sin that a man does is outside the body, but he who commits sexual immorality sins against his own body. Or do you not know that your body is the temple of the Holy Spirit who is in you, whom you have from God, and you are not your own? For you were bought at a price; therefore glorify God in your body and in your spirit, which are God's.

1 Corinthians 6:15–20

Do not lust after her beauty in your heart,
    Nor let her allure you with her eyelids.
For by means of a harlot
    A man is reduced to a crust of bread;
    And an adulteress will prey upon his precious life.

Proverbs 6:25–26

Put off, concerning your former conduct, the old man which grows corrupt according to the deceitful lusts, and be renewed in the spirit of your mind, and . . . put on the new man which was created according to God, in true righteousness and holiness. . . . [Do not] give place to the devil.

Ephesians 4:22–24, 27

Now therefore, listen to me, my children;
    Pay attention to the words of my mouth:
Do not let your heart turn aside to her ways,
    Do not stray into her paths;
For she has cast down many wounded,
    And all who were slain by her were strong men.
Her house is the way to hell,
    Descending to the chambers of death.

Proverbs 7:24–27

If we confess our sins, He is faithful and just to forgive us our sins and to cleanse us from all unrighteousness.

1 John 1:9

When There Is Stress

Be strong and of good courage, do not fear nor be afraid of them; for the Lord your God, He is the One who goes with you. He will not leave you nor forsake you.

Deuteronomy 31:6

The Lord is near to all who call upon Him,
    To all who call upon Him in truth.
He will fulfill the desire of those who fear Him;
    He also will hear their cry and save them.

Psalm 145:18–19

Now may the God of hope fill you with all joy and peace in believing, that you may abound in hope by the power of the Holy Spirit.

Romans 15:13

Peace I leave with you, My peace I give to you; not as the world gives do I give to you. Let not your heart be troubled, neither let it be afraid.

John 14:27

Be anxious for nothing, but in everything by prayer and supplication, with thanksgiving, let your requests be made known to God; and the peace of God, which surpasses all understanding, will guard your hearts and minds through Christ Jesus.

Philippians 4:6–7

You are my hiding place;
    You shall preserve me from trouble;
    You shall surround me with songs of deliverance.
I will instruct you and teach you in the way you should go;
    I will guide you with My eye.

Psalm 32:7–8

For in the time of trouble
    He shall hide me in His pavilion;
    In the secret place of His tabernacle
    He shall hide me;
    He shall set me high upon a rock.

And now my head shall be lifted up above my enemies all
                around me;
    Therefore I will offer sacrifices of joy in His tabernacle;
    I will sing, yes, I will sing praises to the Lord.

Psalm 27:5–6

When There Is Temptation

No temptation has overtaken you except such as is common to man; but God is faithful, who will not allow you to be tempted beyond what you are able, but with the temptation will also make the way of escape, that you may be able to bear it.

1 Corinthians 10:13

Now the Lord is the Spirit; and where the Spirit of the Lord is, there is liberty.

2 Corinthians 3:17

Count it all joy when you fall into various trials.

James 1:2

The Lord knows how to deliver the godly out of temptations and to reserve the unjust under punishment for the day of judgment.

2 Peter 2:9

Keep your heart with all diligence,
    For out of it spring the issues of life.
Put away from you a deceitful mouth,
    And put perverse lips far from you.
Let your eyes look straight ahead,
    And your eyelids look right before you.
Ponder the path of your feet,
    And let all your ways be established.
Do not turn to the right or the left;
    Remove your foot from evil.

Proverbs 4:23–27

Submit to God. Resist the devil and he will flee from you. Draw near to God and He will draw near to you. Cleanse your hands, you sinners; and purify your hearts, you double-minded.

James 4:7–8

This is what [God] commanded them, saying, "Obey My voice, and I will be your God, and you shall be My people. And walk in all the ways that I have commanded you, that it may be well with you."

Jeremiah 7:23

Blessed is the man who endures temptation; for when he has been approved, he will receive the crown of life which the Lord has promised to those who love Him. Let no one say when he is tempted, "I am tempted by God"; for God cannot be tempted by evil, nor does He Himself tempt anyone. But each one is tempted when he is drawn away by his own desires and enticed.

James 1:12–14

When There Is Worry

In righteousness you shall be established;
　　You shall be far from oppression, for you shall not fear;
　　And from terror, for it shall not come near you.

Isaiah 54:14

You have also given me the shield of Your salvation;
　　Your right hand has held me up,
　　Your gentleness has made me great.
You enlarged my path under me,
　　So my feet did not slip.

Psalm 18:35–36

He who dwells in the secret place of the Most High
　　Shall abide under the shadow of the Almighty.
I will say of the LORD, "He is my refuge and my fortress;
　　My God, in Him I will trust."

Psalm 91:1–2

Whoever listens to me will dwell safely,
　　And will be secure, without fear of evil.

Proverbs 1:33

The Lord will deliver me from every evil work and preserve me for His heavenly kingdom. To Him be glory forever and ever. Amen!

2 Timothy 4:18

"No weapon formed against you shall prosper,
>And every tongue which rises against you in judgment
>You shall condemn.
>This is the heritage of the servants of the LORD,
>And their righteousness is from Me,"
>Says the LORD.

Isaiah 54:17

Rest in the LORD, and wait patiently for Him;
>Do not fret because of him who prospers in his way,
>Because of the man who brings wicked schemes to pass.
Cease from anger, and forsake wrath;
>Do not fret—it only causes harm.
For evildoers shall be cut off;
>But those who wait on the LORD,
>They shall inherit the earth.

Psalm 37:7–9

My flesh and my heart fail;
But God is the strength of my heart and my portion
forever. . . .
It is good for me to draw near to God;
I have put my trust in the LORD God,
That I may declare all Your works.

Psalm 73:26, 28

I know the thoughts that I think toward you, says the
LORD, thoughts of peace and not of evil, to give you a future
and a hope.

Jeremiah 29:11

When There Is Worldly Influence

Be strong and of good courage; do not be afraid, nor be dismayed, for the LORD your God is with you wherever you go.

Joshua 1:9

Those who trust in the LORD
   Are like Mount Zion,
   Which cannot be moved, but abides forever.
As the mountains surround Jerusalem,
   So the LORD surrounds His people
   From this time forth and forever. . . .
Do good, O LORD, to those who are good,
   And to those who are upright in their hearts.

Psalm 125:1–2, 4

If anyone desires to come after Me, let him deny himself, and take up his cross daily, and follow Me. For whoever desires to save his life will lose it, but whoever loses his life for My sake will save it.

Luke 9:23–24

This is a faithful saying:

For if we died with Him,
  We shall also live with Him.
If we endure,
  We shall also reign with Him.
If we deny Him,
  He also will deny us.
If we are faithless,
  He remains faithful;
He cannot deny Himself.

2 Timothy 2:11–13

Beloved, we are confident of better things concerning you, yes, things that accompany salvation, though we speak in this manner. For God is not unjust to forget your work and labor of love which you have shown toward His name, in that you have ministered to the saints, and do minister. And we desire that each one of you show the same diligence to the full assurance of hope until the end, that you do not become sluggish, but imitate those who through faith and patience inherit the promises.

Hebrews 6:9–12

Beloved, do not imitate what is evil, but what is good. He who does good is of God, but he who does evil has not seen God.

3 John 11

Do not be conformed to this world, but be transformed by the renewing of your mind, that you may prove what is that good and acceptable and perfect will of God.

Romans 12:2

God's
Desires

Compassion in Marriage

All of you be of one mind, having compassion for one another; love as brothers, be tenderhearted, be courteous; not returning evil for evil or reviling for reviling, but on the contrary blessing, knowing that you were called to this, that you may inherit a blessing.

1 Peter 3:8–9

Whatever you do, do it heartily, as to the Lord and not to men, knowing that from the Lord you will receive the reward of the inheritance; for you serve the Lord Christ. But he who does wrong will be repaid for what he has done, and there is no partiality.

Colossians 3:23–25

Command those who are rich in this present age not to be haughty, nor to trust in uncertain riches but in the living God, who gives us richly all things to enjoy. Let them do good, that they be rich in good works, ready to give, willing to share, storing up for themselves a good foundation for the time to come, that they may lay hold on eternal life.

1 Timothy 6:17–19

He who finds his life will lose it, and he who loses his life for My sake will find it.

Matthew 10:39

All the brothers of the poor hate him;
  How much more do his friends go far from him!
  He may pursue them with words, yet they
          abandon him.

Proverbs 19:7

By this all will know that you are My disciples, if you have love for one another.

John 13:35

So the people asked [John the Baptist], saying, "What shall we do then?" He answered and said to them, "He who has two tunics, let him give to him who has none; and he who has food, let him do likewise."

Luke 3:10–11

Whoever desires to be first among you, let him be your slave—just as the Son of Man did not come to be served, but to serve, and to give His life a ransom for many.

Matthew 20:27–28

 Commitment in Marriage

Whatever you do, do it heartily, as to the Lord and not to men, knowing that from the Lord you will receive the reward of the inheritance; for you serve the Lord Christ.

Colossians 3:23–24

I thank my God upon every remembrance of you . . . being confident of this very thing, that He who has begun a good work in you will complete it until the day of Jesus Christ.

Philippians 1:3, 6

Let us not grow weary while doing good, for in due season we shall reap if we do not lose heart. Therefore, as we have opportunity, let us do good to all, especially to those who are of the household of faith.

Galatians 6:9–10

When you make a vow to God, do not delay to pay it;
    For He has no pleasure in fools.
    Pay what you have vowed—
Better not to vow than to vow and not pay.

Ecclesiastes 5:4–5

When [Jesus] had called the people to Himself, with His disciples also, He said to them, "Whoever desires to come after Me, let him deny himself, and take up his cross, and follow Me. For whoever desires to save his life will lose it, but whoever loses his life for My sake and the gospel's will save it. For what will it profit a man if he gains the whole world, and loses his own soul? Or what will a man give in exchange for his soul?"

Mark 8:34–37

Let none deal treacherously with the wife of his youth.
   For the LORD God of Israel says
    That He hates divorce.

Malachi 2:15–16

No temptation has overtaken you except such as is common to man; but God is faithful, who will not allow you to be tempted beyond what you are able, but with the temptation will also make the way of escape, that you may be able to bear it.

1 Corinthians 10:13

Contentment in Marriage

We know that all things work together for good to those who love God, to those who are the called according to His purpose.

Romans 8:28

Let your conduct be without covetousness; be content with such things as you have. For He Himself has said, "I will never leave you nor forsake you." So we may boldly say:

"The LORD is my helper;
I will not fear.
What can man do to me?"

Hebrews 13:5–6

Now godliness with contentment is great gain. For we brought nothing into this world, and it is certain we can carry nothing out. And having food and clothing, with these we shall be content.

1 Timothy 6:6–8

Do not worry, saying, "What shall we eat?" or "What shall we drink?" or "What shall we wear?" For after all these things the Gentiles seek. For your heavenly Father knows that you need all these things. But seek first the kingdom of God and His righteousness, and all these things shall be added to you. Therefore do not worry about tomorrow, for tomorrow will worry about its own things. Sufficient for the day is its own trouble.

Matthew 6:31–34

Not that I speak in regard to need, for I have learned in whatever state I am, to be content: I know how to be abased, and I know how to abound. Everywhere and in all things I have learned both to be full and to be hungry, both to abound and to suffer need. I can do all things through Christ who strengthens me.

Philippians 4:11–13

Thus says the LORD:
    "Stand in the ways and see,
    And ask for the old paths, where the good way is,
    And walk in it;
    Then you will find rest for your souls."

Jeremiah 6:16

Delight yourself also in the LORD,
And He shall give you the desires of your heart.

Commit your way to the LORD,
Trust also in Him,
And He shall bring it to pass.
He shall bring forth your righteousness as the light,
And your justice as the noonday.

Psalm 37:4–6

Endurance in Marriage

Blessed is the man who endures temptation; for when he has been approved, he will receive the crown of life which the Lord has promised to those who love Him.... Therefore submit to God. Resist the devil and he will flee from you.

James 1:12; 4:7

Since we are surrounded by so great a cloud of witnesses, let us lay aside every weight, and the sin which so easily ensnares us, and let us run with endurance the race that is set before us, looking unto Jesus, the author and finisher of our faith, who for the joy that was set before Him endured the cross, despising the shame, and has sat down at the right hand of the throne of God.

Hebrews 12:1–2

He who dwells in the secret place of the Most High
    Shall abide under the shadow of the Almighty.
I will say of the Lord, "He is my refuge and my fortress;
    My God, in Him I will trust."

Psalm 91:1–2

The Lord upholds all who fall,
And raises up all who are bowed down.
　The eyes of all look expectantly to You,
And You give them their food in due season.
　You open Your hand
And satisfy the desire of every living thing.

Psalm 145:14–16

Indeed we count them blessed who endure. You have heard of the perseverance of Job and seen the end intended by the Lord—that the Lord is very compassionate and merciful.

James 5:11

He knows the way that I take;
　When He has tested me, I shall come forth as gold.

Job 23:10

You, O God, have tested us;
　You have refined us as silver is refined.

Psalm 66:10

Forgiveness in Marriage

Let all bitterness, wrath, anger, clamor, and evil speaking be put away from you, with all malice. And be kind to one another, tenderhearted, forgiving one another, even as God in Christ forgave you.

Ephesians 4:31–32

If you forgive men their trespasses, your heavenly Father will also forgive you. But if you do not forgive men their trespasses, neither will your Father forgive your trespasses.

Matthew 6:14–15

Then Peter came to [Jesus] and said, "Lord, how often shall my brother sin against me, and I forgive him? Up to seven times?"

Jesus said to him, "I do not say to you, up to seven times, but up to seventy times seven."

Matthew 18:21–22

Take heed to yourselves. If your brother sins against you, rebuke him; and if he repents, forgive him.

Luke 17:3

Whenever you stand praying, if you have anything against anyone, forgive him, that your Father in heaven may also forgive you your trespasses.

Mark 11:25

[Bear] with one another, and [forgive] one another, if anyone has a complaint against another; even as Christ forgave you, so you also must do.

Colossians 3:13

Bless the Lord, O my soul,
    And forget not all His benefits:
Who forgives all your iniquities,
    Who heals all your diseases,
Who redeems your life from destruction,
    Who crowns you with lovingkindness and tender
                mercies,
Who satisfies your mouth with good things,
    So that your youth is renewed like the eagle's.

Psalm 103:2–5

Generosity in Marriage

He who has a generous eye will be blessed,
For he gives of his bread to the poor.

Proverbs 22:9

Give, and it will be given to you: good measure, pressed down, shaken together, and running over will be put into your bosom. For with the same measure that you use, it will be measured back to you.

Luke 6:38

The generous soul will be made rich,
And he who waters will also be watered himself.

Proverbs 11:25

He who sows sparingly will also reap sparingly, and he who sows bountifully will also reap bountifully. So let each one give as he purposes in his heart, not grudgingly or of necessity; for God loves a cheerful giver.

2 Corinthians 9:6–7

Do not lay up for yourselves treasures on earth, where moth and rust destroy and where thieves break in and steal; but lay up for yourselves treasures in heaven, where neither moth nor rust destroys and where thieves do not break in and steal. For where your treasure is, there your heart will be also.

Matthew 6:19–21

Give to the LORD the glory due His name;
    Bring an offering, and come into His courts.

Psalm 96:8

A generous man devises generous things,
    And by generosity he shall stand.

Isaiah 32:8

He who is faithful in what is least is faithful also in much; and he who is unjust in what is least is unjust also in much.

Luke 16:10

Whatever you want men to do to you, do also to them.

Matthew 7:12

Honesty in Marriage

Let no corrupt word proceed out of your mouth, but what is good for necessary edification, that it may impart grace to the hearers. . . .

Let all bitterness, wrath, anger, clamor, and evil speaking be put away from you, with all malice. And be kind to one another, tenderhearted, forgiving one another, even as God in Christ forgave you.

Ephesians 4:29, 31–32

Putting away lying, "Let each one of you speak truth with his neighbor," for we are members of one another.

Ephesians 4:25

Pleasant words are like a honeycomb,
Sweetness to the soul and health to the bones.

Proverbs 16:24

The truthful lip shall be established forever,
But a lying tongue is but for a moment.

Proverbs 12:19

A good man out of the good treasure of his heart brings forth good; and an evil man out of the evil treasure of his heart brings forth evil. For out of the abundance of the heart his mouth speaks.

Luke 6:45

Whoever guards his mouth and tongue
    Keeps his soul from troubles.

Proverbs 21:23

Death and life are in the power of the tongue,
    And those who love it will eat its fruit.

Proverbs 18:21

Humility in Marriage

I will praise the name of God with a song,
　　And will magnify Him with thanksgiving.
This also shall please the LORD better than an ox or bull,
　　Which has horns and hooves.
The humble shall see this and be glad;
　　And you who seek God, your hearts shall live.

Psalm 69:30–32

Who is wise and understanding among you? Let him show by good conduct that his works are done in the meekness of wisdom.

James 3:13

Pride goes before destruction,
　　And a haughty spirit before a fall.
Better to be of a humble spirit with the lowly,
　　Than to divide the spoil with the proud.
He who heeds the word wisely will find good,
　　And whoever trusts in the Lord, happy is he.

Proverbs 16:18–20

He who is of a proud heart stirs up strife,
But he who trusts in the Lord will be prospered.
He who trusts in his own heart is a fool,
But whoever walks wisely will be delivered.

Proverbs 28:25–26

Likewise you younger people, submit yourselves to your elders. Yes, all of you be submissive to one another, and be clothed with humility, for

"God resists the proud,
But gives grace to the humble."

Therefore humble yourselves under the mighty hand of God, that He may exalt you in due time.

1 Peter 5:5–6

Whoever desires to become great among you, let him be your servant. And whoever desires to be first among you, let him be your slave.

Matthew 20:26–27

The fear of the LORD is the instruction of wisdom,
And before honor is humility.

Proverbs 15:33

Take My yoke upon you and learn from Me, for I am gentle and lowly in heart, and you will find rest for your souls. For My yoke is easy and My burden is light.

Matthew 11:29–30

Let nothing be done through selfish ambition or conceit, but in lowliness of mind let each esteem others better than himself. Let each of you look out not only for his own interests, but also for the interests of others.

Philippians 2:3–4

Love in Marriage

Let love be without hypocrisy. Abhor what is evil. Cling to what is good. Be kindly affectionate to one another with brotherly love, in honor giving preference to one another.

Romans 12:9–10

Be imitators of God as dear children. And walk in love, as Christ also has loved us and given Himself for us, an offering and a sacrifice to God for a sweet-smelling aroma.

Ephesians 5:1–2

Put on love, which is the bond of perfection.

Colossians 3:14

We have known and believed the love that God has for us. God is love, and he who abides in love abides in God, and God in him. . . . We love Him because He first loved us.

1 John 4:16, 19

I love those who love me,
 And those who seek me diligently will find me.

Proverbs 8:17

Beloved, let us love one another, for love is of God; and everyone who loves is born of God and knows God. He who does not love does not know God, for God is love. In this the love of God was manifested toward us, that God has sent His only begotten Son into the world, that we might live through Him. In this is love, not that we loved God, but that He loved us and sent His Son to be the propitiation for our sins. Beloved, if God so loved us, we also ought to love one another.

No one has seen God at any time. If we love one another, God abides in us, and His love has been perfected in us.

1 John 4:7–12

As the Father loved Me, I also have loved you; abide in My love. If you keep My commandments, you will abide in My love, just as I have kept My Father's commandments and abide in His love. These things I have spoken to you, that My joy may remain in you, and that your joy may be full. This is My commandment, that you love one another as I have loved you. Greater love has no one than this, than to lay down one's life for his friends. . . . These things I command you, that you love one another.

John 15:9–13, 17

He who has My commandments and keeps them, it is he who loves Me. And he who loves Me will be loved by My Father, and I will love him and manifest Myself to him.

John 14:21

Love suffers long and is kind; love does not envy; love does not parade itself, is not puffed up; does not behave rudely, does not seek its own, is not provoked, thinks no evil; does not rejoice in iniquity, but rejoices in the truth; bears all things, believes all things, hopes all things, endures all things. Love never fails.

1 Corinthians 13:4–8

Purity in Marriage

Blessed are the pure in heart,
　　For they shall see God.
Blessed are the peacemakers,
　　For they shall be called sons of God.
Blessed are those who are persecuted for righteousness'
　　　　　　　sake,
　　For theirs is the kingdom of heaven.

Matthew 5:8–10

Brethren, whatever things are true, whatever things are noble, whatever things are just, whatever things are pure, whatever things are lovely, whatever things are of good report, if there is any virtue and if there is anything praise-worthy—meditate on these things.

Philippians 4:8

[Do] nothing with partiality. Do not lay hands on anyone hastily, nor share in other people's sins; keep yourself pure.

1 Timothy 5:21–22

Beloved, now we are children of God; and it has not yet been revealed what we shall be, but we know that when He is revealed, we shall be like Him, for we shall see Him as He is. And everyone who has this hope in Him purifies himself, just as He is pure.

1 John 3:2–3

The wisdom that is from above is first pure, then peaceable, gentle, willing to yield, full of mercy and good fruits, without partiality and without hypocrisy. Now the fruit of righteousness is sown in peace by those who make peace.

James 3:17–18

Let no one despise your youth, but be an example to the believers in word, in conduct, in love, in spirit, in faith, in purity.

1 Timothy 4:12

May [you] become blameless and harmless, children of God without fault in the midst of a crooked and perverse generation, among whom you shine as lights in the world, holding fast the word of life, so that I may rejoice in the day of Christ that I have not run in vain or labored in vain.

Philippians 2:15–16

Steadfastness in Marriage

One thing I do, forgetting those things which are behind and reaching forward to those things which are ahead, I press toward the goal for the prize of the upward call of God in Christ Jesus.

Philippians 3:13–14

As long as my breath is in me,
 And the breath of God in my nostrils,
My lips will not speak wickedness,
 Nor my tongue utter deceit.

Job 27:3–4

He knows the way that I take;
 When He has tested me, I shall come forth as gold.
My foot has held fast to His steps;
 I have kept His way and not turned aside.

Job 23:10–11

I will instruct you and teach you in the way you should go;
I will guide you with My eye.

Psalm 32:8

Be steadfast, immovable, always abounding in the work of the Lord, knowing that your labor is not in vain in the Lord.

1 Corinthians 15:58

Be sober, be vigilant; because your adversary the devil walks about like a roaring lion, seeking whom he may devour. Resist him, steadfast in the faith, knowing that the same sufferings are experienced by your brotherhood in the world.

1 Peter 5:8–9

Praise the LORD!
    Blessed is the man who fears the Lord,
    Who delights greatly in His commandments.

Psalm 112:1

I can do all things through Christ who strengthens me.

Philippians 4:13

He who has begun a good work in you will complete it until the day of Jesus Christ.

Philippians 1:6

GOD'S DESIRES

 # Thoughtfulness in Marriage

Giving all diligence, add to your faith virtue, to virtue knowledge, to knowledge self-control, to self-control perseverance, to perseverance godliness, to godliness brotherly kindness, and to brotherly kindness love.

2 Peter 1:5–7

You must support the weak. And remember the words of the Lord Jesus, that He said, "It is more blessed to give than to receive."

Acts 20:35

Walk in love, as Christ also has loved us and given Himself for us, an offering and a sacrifice to God for a sweet-smelling aroma.

Ephesians 5:2

Let no one seek his own, but each one the other's well-being.

1 Corinthians 10:24

Now may the God of patience and comfort grant you to be like-minded toward one another, according to Christ Jesus, that you may with one mind and one mouth glorify the God and Father of our Lord Jesus Christ.

Therefore receive one another, just as Christ also received us, to the glory of God.

Romans 15:5–7

Love suffers long and is kind; love does not envy; love does not parade itself, is not puffed up; does not behave rudely, does not seek its own, is not provoked, thinks no evil; does not rejoice in iniquity, but rejoices in the truth; bears all things, believes all things, hopes all things, endures all things.

1 Corinthians 13:4–7

Whatever you want men to do to you, do also to them.

Matthew 7:12

Notes

Notes

Notes

Notes

Notes

Notes

Notes

Notes

Notes

Notes